W9-ASG-151

JAN 1978
RECEIVED
OHIO DOMINICAN
COLLEGE LIBRARY
COLUMBUS, OHIO

Twayne's English Authors Series

Cyril Tourneur

TEAS 221

This emblem, from Peacham's *Minerva Britanna,* depicts visually two of the themes—death and earthly love—which dominate the works of the Jacobean dramatists and, particularly, Cyril Tourneur.

CYRIL TOURNEUR

By SAMUEL SCHUMAN

University of Maine, Orono

TWAYNE PUBLISHERS
A DIVISION OF G. K. HALL & CO., BOSTON

822.3
T728 S
1977

Copyright © 1977 by G. K. Hall & Co.
All Rights Reserved
First Printing

Library of Congress Cataloging in Publication Data

Schuman, Samuel.
  Cyril Tourneur.

  (Twayne's English authors series ; TEAS 221)
  Bibliography: p. 157–61
  Includes index.
  1. Tourneur, Cyril, 1575?–1626—Criticism and
interpretation.
PR3174.S3   822'.3   77-21369
ISBN 0-8057-6690-1

MANUFACTURED IN THE UNITED STATES OF AMERICA

For Nancy, Daniel, and Leah.

103525

Contents

About the Author

Samuel Schuman is a native of Glencoe, Illinois. He holds the BA degree from Grinnell College with "distinction," the MA from San Francisco State College with "Honors," and the PhD from Northwestern University, where his dissertation, under the direction of Jean Hagstrum and Samuel Schoenbaum, was entitled "The Theater of Fine Devices: Emblems and the Emblematic in the Plays of John Webster." In addition to the dissertation, Dr. Schuman has published numerous articles on the subject of the Renaissance Drama, with a particular concentration upon the relationship between the stage and the visual arts, in such journals as *Texas Studies in Literature and Language*, *Notes and Queries*, and *Modern Philology*. He has served as Assistant Editor of *Renaissance Drama*, an annual published by the Northwestern University Press, and *Research Opportunities in Renaissance Drama*, the report of the Modern Language Association Conference. Although Dr. Schuman's scholarly activities have centered upon the Jacobean stage, he has not been confined to this area: his published works have also focused upon such diverse topics as *The Wizard of Oz*, Chaucer's *Troilus and Criseyde*, Vladimir Nabokov's *Invitation to a Beheading*, and Robert Heinlein's "They."

Dr. Schuman is an active member of the Modern Language Association of America, the American Association of University Professors, and the National and Iowa Conferences of Teachers of English. He recently traveled in England with the aid of a Ford Foundation Humanities Grant.

Dr. Schuman began his teaching career at St. Mary's College in California, and has taught at Cornell College, Mt. Vernon, Iowa, where, in addition to his classroom duties he directed several Elizabethan plays.

He is currently Director of the Honors Program at the University of Maine, Orono.

Preface

If we have learned anything from the horrors of our century, it is the relevance of a literature which insists upon finding "some pattern of ethical causality in the loathsome."[1] The Jacobean drama is such a literature, and there is no playwright of this period less relenting in his pursuit of the loathsome than Cyril Tourneur. Tourneur's works present a world in which man's inhumanity to man is overshadowed only by the ultimate inhumanity of ever-present death. It is a real world, and, at least some of the time, we live in it. It can be unpleasant to study Tourneur; but the more our world comes to resemble the nightmare vision of Tourneur's stage, the more necessary it becomes to do so.

It is the aim of this work to present the poems and plays of Cyril Tourneur within the frame of the contemporary literary and historical situation, and with reference to what we can reconstruct of Tourneur's own biography. The following pages are based on the belief that a consideration of Tourneur's life—as soldier, diplomat, and professional playwright—is important in understanding the genesis of his works, and that the historical and social movements of his time helped to generate his life. Although the works ultimately stand or fall by themselves (like Tourneur's characters), each one also casts light on the others and is in turn illuminated by the rest of the canon. Thus, for example, Tourneur's two major plays—*The Revenger's Tragedy* and *The Atheist's Tragedy*—are universally recognized as dealing with the theme of death; but it is curious how little attention has been paid to the fact that three of his minor works are elegies. The consideration of Tourneur's plays and poems in the context of their biographical, historical, and literary background has led to some general conclusions about the meaning and importance of his extant works taken as a whole.

The belief that each of Tourneur's writings, while ultimately an individualized work of art, is best understood within the multiple contexts of the author's life, times, and inherited literary traditions, dictates the structure of the chapters which follow. Chapter 1 is a brief consideration of the life of Tourneur—what little is known of it—and the historical milieu in which it took place. Since our knowledge of Tourneur's life is so sketchy, an unusual amount of attention is paid to defining the perimeters within which he functioned. If we do not know what Tourneur did as a soldier, for example, we do know what Renaissance soldiers did. Social history, particularly as it reflects the military and artistic community in which Tourneur lived his life, is considered of equal importance with political history. The next five chapters are devoted to an analysis of Tourneur's works, major and minor, with particular consideration being given to the literary traditions out of which they arose and to which they contributed. Special attention is paid to the traditions of the medieval moralities, Renaissance satire, and the tragedy of revenge. Since Tourneur's works exhibit a steady development, they are discussed in the order in which they are generally assumed to have been composed. The present writer does not believe that this development hinges upon *The Revenger's Tragedy*. Since the authorship of this work—if Tourneur's, his greatest—is subject to serious question, any general statement about Tourneur which depends heavily upon *The Revenger's Tragedy* is dangerous, and no such statements are made. At the same time, there is a very good chance that Tourneur did write *The Revenger's Tragedy*, and this possibility is taken into account. Since the question of doubtful authorship is vital to a consideration of *The Revenger's Tragedy*, one chapter is devoted to this issue, another to the nature of the work itself. These two subjects should not be confused.

Each work has been allocated space roughly proportionate to its importance. While some comparative observations and judgments are offered during the discussion of particular works, generalizations concerning the entire Tourneur canon are left for the concluding chapter.

No systematic attempt has been made to present an historical overview of Tourneur critics and criticism. Tourneur has frequently merited a comment, but only infrequently been a central focus of scholarly attention. It would be a disservice to all concerned to study many of the hasty citations of Tourneur made by notable scholars and critics on the way to some point quite irrelevant to Tourneur studies. The reader who wishes to undertake such a survey might find the appended selected Bibliography a helpful beginning. It is hoped that the majority will not be dissatisfied with its selectivity.

SAMUEL SCHUMAN

The University of Maine at Orono

Acknowledgments

That I have been able to complete this book and come up with any conclusions at all is due in no small part to the unselfish assistance provided by the libraries within which I have worked, and the even more selfless cooperation of the colleagues and students with whom I have labored. I have especially to thank my typist, factotum, and friend, Ms Ruth Jennings Nellis. It is more difficult to list those teachers, friends, and colleagues without whose encouragement and instruction I might never have started. I am particularly grateful to Dr. Samuel Schoenbaum, who introduced me to the Jacobean drama, and Dr. Ruby Cohn, who taught me the methodology of literary study, and some of the humane reasons for undertaking such investigation in the first place. My greatest debt is acknowledged, but not paid, in the dedication.

Chronology

ca. 1580 Cyril Tourneur born, perhaps in Essex.

1596 Possibly joins an expedition to Cadiz, led by Essex and Drake, and accompanied by Sir Christopher Heydon and Sir Francis Vere, both of whom are later associated with Tourneur. At about this time, Tourneur serves as secretary to Sir Francis Vere.

1600 Publishes *The Transformed Metamorphosis*.

1605 *Laugh and Lie Down: or, the World's Folly*, signed "C. T." and attributed to Tourneur.

1606 Probable year of composition and production of *The Revenger's Tragedy*.

1607 October 7, *The Revenger's Tragedy* entered on the Stationers' Register. Published later in the year.

1608 August 28, Sir Francis Vere dies.

1609 *A Funeral Poem upon the death of the Most Worthy and True Soldier, Sir Francis Vere*.

ca. 1610 *The Atheist's Tragedy* written and performed.

1611 September 14, *The Atheist's Tragedy* entered on the Stationers' Register.

1612 February 15, Tourneur's lost play, *The Nobleman*, is entered on the Stationers' Register and recorded in the Revels list as performed at court by the King's Men on February 23 and again at Christmas. Tourneur writes the *Character of Robert, Earl of Salisbury*, who died in May, and *A Grief on the Death of Prince Henry*, who died on November 6.

1613 *A Grief on the Death of Prince Henry* is printed in *Three Elegies on the Most Lamented Death of Prince Henry*. June 15, Robert Daborne writes Phillip Henslowe that he has "given Cyrill Tourneur an act of the Arreignment of London to write." In December, it is probable Tourneur gives up his career as a writer and resumes work as a diplomat, carrying official papers from London to Brussels.

1617   September 1, arrested for unknown reasons and released on October 18 to the custody of Sir Edward Cecil.

1625   August 2–September 26, serves as secretary to the council of war. October 8, joins the attack on Cadiz as secretary to Cecil. December 11, following the failure of the expedition, Tourneur is put off his ship, mortally ill, at Kinsale, Ireland.

1626   Tourneur dies on February 18 at Kinsale.

1632   Tourneur's widow, Mary, petitions the council of war for her late husband's pay, pleading her poverty.

CHAPTER 1

Life and Times

I Beginnings

IT is impossible to stretch the extant facts of Cyril Tourneur's life into the outline of a normal biography. What is known is both sparse and unrelated: we know, for instance, the financial condition of Tourneur's widow six years after her husband's death—but that is our first record or even hint that he was married. We are quite certain regarding the date and facts of Tourneur's death—his birth and the first half of his life are a complete mystery. It is perhaps appropriate to draw a quick breath of fact before we plunge into the murky obscurity of conjecture: in 1600, there appeared an allegorical verse satire entitled "The Transformed Metamorphosis. By Cyril Turner."[1] This is Tourneur's first published work, and it is also the first historical record of his existence. Using *The Transformed Metamorphosis* as a kind of fulcrum, we can try to project what came before on the basis of what came after.

Cyril Tourneur was probably born between 1575 and 1585. There are several points on which this conjecture is based. *The Transformed Metamorphosis* itself seems to be the work of a young man. The dark satire of the poem and its chaotic rhetoric are perfectly in keeping with "a fashion which swept much of the poetic youth of England into its net."[2] While the attempt to be up-to-date need not necessarily reflect youth, it is more often found in an artist in his second or third decade than in his fifth or sixth. Moreover, the later Tourneur, the author of *The Revenger's Tragedy* and *The Atheist's Tragedy*, seems much more a man to set fashions than to follow them.

Other known facts of Tourneur's life argue for a birthdate around 1580. For example, in 1625 Tourneur sailed with an expedition to attack Cadiz. On this voyage, Tourneur served in the capacity of

15

secretary to the court of Lord Marshall Sir Edward Cecil. While the importance of the post suggests a mature man, the nature of the mission equally strongly suggests that in 1625 Tourneur was not in his dotage. Weak old men are not often sent along, even as clerical functionaries, on long and demanding sea voyages.

Tourneur, then, was probably about twenty years old when *The Transformed Metamorphosis* was published, about forty-five when he undertook the expedition to Cadiz. If we can guess with some confidence about when Tourneur was born much less certainty is possible in establishing his ancestry. Indeed, the safest conclusion to draw is that we simply do not know who Tourneur's parents were, or where they lived. This is not for lack of candidates—there are numerous Tourneurs (or Tournours or Turners or Turnors) to be found in the records of Elizabethan society. Unfortunately, none of these families seems to have any strong demonstrable connection with our Cyril Tourneur. There is, however, one family of Turnors with whom some extremely tenuous links have been suggested, and since the possibility of a family is better (or at least more satisying to the biographer) than no family at all, these links are worth noting.

There is a great deal of evidence, some of it from his own hand, that Tourneur was for a long time a servant of the Cecil family, and of Sir Francis Vere. Tourneur wrote a "Character"[3] of Robert Cecil, and a funeral poem for Sir Francis Vere. The Cecils provided bail when Tourneur was arrested. Furthermore, since Tourneur was granted a pension of sixty pounds from the United Provinces, we may assume that he served Vere and the Cecils for at least some time in the Netherlands where, in fact, Vere spent most of his active career.

These facts are important, for there is another Tourneur (or, in this case, Turnor) who also served these men, at this time, and in this place. Captain Richard Turnor had a minor political appointment under Sir Thomas Cecil in the Dutch town of Brill, and later he became the lieutenant governor of that town. He served in this capacity until Sir Francis Vere became governor in 1598 and was then replaced.

While there is no proof that Cyril Tourneur and Richard Turnor had any connection with each other at all, it should be remembered that, in Elizabethan England, certain sorts of occupations and associations tended to run in families. A soldier or minor diplomat would almost certainly have a father or brothers or sons or cousins who were also soldiers or minor diplomats. A servant of the Cecils would almost certainly have among his relations other servants of the Cecils. Given this inclination toward hereditary patterns of life, it seems at least possible that Cyril Tourneur was connected with the family of Captain Richard Turnor.

We do know something about this Turnor family, due to one of those historical accidents that make family chroniclers out of otherwise sane men. When Captain Richard Turnor was dismissed by Sir Francis Vere as lieutenant governor of Brill, Richard's brother Edward Turnor wrote a letter to try to have his brother reinstated, and that letter has survived. In it, Edward identifies himself as a member of the Middle Temple,[4] an institution which kept careful records concerning the families of its constituents. From these records, we learn that Richard and Edward Turnor's father was another Edward Turnor, of Canons, Essex, who was married twice and had at least nine children. Two facts here seem to argue some possible connection between this family of Turnors and Cyril Tourneur. First, Essex is the home of the Cecils. Second, the Turnors of Canons, Essex, had a penchant for just the sort of exotic Christian name of which "Cyril" is a good example. This Turnor family includes among its members a Penelope, a Lydia, a Demetrius (all three Greek, like "Cyril") as well as a Thomasina, a Debora, and a Maurice.

Here this particular chain of speculation ends. The reader may judge for himself whether all these weak links make a feasible chain. The most reasonable conclusion would seem to be that, while there are no good nominees for Cyril Tourneur's family and birthplace, the Edward Turnor family of Essex seems a better guess than any other.

II *Historical Background*

We can estimate when Tourneur was born, and can only guess where and of what family. On the other hand, we know a great deal about the world into which he was born. To understand Tourneur's life as both poet and civil servant, we must briefly consider the historical background against which this life unfolded.

Cyril Tourneur grew up in the 1580s and 1590s, the last two decades of Elizabethan England. The history of this period is largely the history of Elizabeth and her maritime policy.

Elizabeth was the last of the Tudor monarchs, three of whom

ruled England for most of the time between 1485 and 1603 (Henry
VII, Henry VIII, and Elizabeth herself). She became queen in
1558, and ruled until her death in 1603. During Elizabeth's reign,
England's role in the Western world underwent a profound change.
In a seemingly paradoxical fashion, in the last years of the sixteenth
century, England became both insular and imperialistic. Elizabeth's
father, Henry VIII, had, at least early in his reign, attempted to
make England a major force in European political life. As a symbolic
example, there had been a major attempt in 1521 to elevate Cardi-
nal Wolsey, Henry's principal advisor, to the papal throne. As the
Henrician reformation gained impetus, however, the king seems to
have become less concerned with aggressive and forceful penetra-
tion into the European sphere, and more concerned with diplomatic
means of acquiring and keeping power. His marriage in 1540 to
Anne of Cleves—"casting about for an ally, as much as searching for
a bride"5—is a good example of this sort of political maneuvering.

It was Elizabeth, however, who refined the new notions of
Anglo-European diplomacy into a fine art. The virgin queen mas-
tered the tactic of maintaining a European balance of power in such
a way as to keep Europe internally divided, and hence, out of England's way. France and Spain dominated the continent during
Elizabeth's life, and her foreign policy, reduced to its simplest out-
lines, was to keep those two powers more or less equal by always
coming to the aid of the weaker party, until the balance shifted, at
which time, England's sympathies and aid would simultaneously
shift also. Thus, in the years immediately after Elizabeth's corona-
tion, "Phillip of Spain protected the new Queen's accession and
extended his protection for years after she had fulfilled his worst
fears on the score of religion."6 Yet, by 1572, Elizabeth allowed a
younger brother of King Charles IX of France, Francis, the duke of
Alencon, to consider himself her suitor; in the Elizabethan court,
such social affiliations were inevitably central symbols of formal
political alliances. This contradictory behavior is explained by a shift
in the balance of power: Spain was on the rise, and now England's
duty was to bolster France. For almost half a century, Elizabeth
preserved British independence and power by diplomatic means,
employing weapons ranging from the threat of her armies to the
promise of her hand in marriage.

By the end of Elizabeth's reign, it was no longer necessary to walk this political tightrope as carefully, since by then, England had had time to develop, unobstructed, that weapon which was to remain her greatest strength until this century: her navy. By the time Elizabeth died, England was the unchallenged sea power of the world. England had several natural advantages over Spain and France in the race for control of the oceans, advantages which Elizabeth's protectionist foreign policy allowed the country to develop to the full.

To begin with, England is an island. Most of its inhabitants have always lived within easy reach of the sea. London is a port city, or at least, through the Thames, has a port. Both Spain and France, with inland capitals, have always lacked the sea consciousness of Britain. An English parliamentarian took (and still can take) a boat to go to a meeting of Parliament—his French or Spanish counterpart went overland.

Spain and France have a Mediterranean as well as an Atlantic coast. And since, from a sixteenth-century perspective, the Mediterranean had always been the main water trade route of Europe, both countries thought in terms of a relatively calm, small sea in the development of their naval resources. England, on the other hand, has only the north Atlantic and the North Sea on which to sail, and was therefore forced to develop oceangoing sailors and ships. When the mastery of the oceans became more important than mastery of the Mediterranean, England clearly found its old liability a new asset.

While England's rivals, particularly Spain, exploited their Atlantic capacities for short-term plunder, England developed an import and export trade which was to prove far more durable and even profitable. And protection for this trade was provided by leaders like Hawkins and Drake, who helped to develop an efficient naval force and a professional navy: the ship, its crew, and its military hardware became a weapon. The French and Spanish, however, relying upon their Mediterranean tradition, saw ships and sailors as a means of sea transport for real soldiers—soldiers who proved to be only so much extra baggage in a naval war.[7]

England's major Elizabethan naval hero is, of course, Sir Francis Drake. In 1580, at about the time Tourneur was born, Drake returned from the famous voyage on which he plundered Spanish South America. Drake's voyage served notice to the Spaniards that

England had no intention of allowing Spanish domination of the high seas. Moreover, it demonstrated to the entire world that England felt herself strong enough to take on any comers on the sea. Seven years after Drake plundered South America, he again caught the Spanish navy by surprise, sailing around the coast of Portugal and making a "brilliant dash into Cadiz Harbor on 19–20 April which cost Spain some thirty ships and a quarter of a million ducats, and a loss of prestige and morale not to be measured in figures."[8] There were other expeditions to Cadiz, notably in 1596 and 1625, which tried to duplicate Drake's "singeing of the King of Spain's beard," but none was so successful. Cyril Tourneur was present on the latter of these expeditions, and perhaps the earlier as well.

In 1587, on February 8, England took another step toward overt war with Spain with the execution of Mary, Queen of Scots. Elizabeth's Roman Catholic kinswoman had been in England, in one state of imprisonment or another, for nineteen years. During that time she had perpetually schemed to take the throne from Elizabeth. Mary had been kept alive for mixed reasons, after crimes which would have condemned any other person in England (save the queen herself) to death. Perhaps Elizabeth had some tender feelings of family or regal loyalty. Mary was, after all, a cousin and a queen. More likely, Mary was preserved as a useful pawn in Elizabeth's diplomatic program, since both France and Spain, as Catholic powers, were intensely interested in Mary's welfare and potential claim to the crown. But, in the 1580s, pressure for Mary's execution had become too great—and motives for keeping her alive too few—for Elizabeth to procrastinate any longer.

Finally, in 1588, Spain struck back. The story of the defeat of the Spanish Armada is too familiar to repeat in detail here. The Spanish plan of attack, which involved sailing through the English Channel and disembarking an invading army, was probably not wise. The Spanish general in charge of the entire operation, the duke of Medina Sidonia, was definitely not wise. The Spanish ships were heavy and clumsy compared to their English counterparts, and were also comparatively undermanned. Ultimately, of course, the Spanish were unlucky as well as foolish, always a fatal combination. The weather rendered the Spanish ships helpless—those which were not wrecked—and the English harried the survivors. The

Spanish fled back to Spain, but less than half the ships remained—and less than a third of the men.

From 1587 until 1603 open war raged between England and Spain on land and sea. The sea war took place mostly in Spanish waters; improbably enough, "the chief theatre on land was the Netherlands."[9] It was, almost certainly, in that war between the Dutch Republic and the Spanish Netherlands, that Cyril Tourneur became a soldier.

III   *The War in the Netherlands and Sir Francis Vere*

From 1589 until well into the first decade of the 1600s, Tourneur's first mentor, Sir Francis Vere, acted "in command of all her majesty's soldiers out of the garrisons in the Netherlands."[10] He was also one of England's major diplomatic ambassadors to this troubled area during these years. Thus, when we first meet a historically verifiable Tourneur, he is already a career military servant and diplomat.

Two important documents written by Tourneur himself confirm (although they do not prove) our conjectures concerning his activities during these years. The first of these documents is Tourneur's *Funeral Poem on the Death of Sir Francis Vere*. As we shall see later, this work argues some personal relationship, although no intimacy, between author and subject. Second, Tourneur included in *The Atheist's Tragedy* a rather lengthy and detailed description of the siege of Ostend. It was Vere who managed the rather heroic and well planned defense of that Dutch city. Finally, in 1614, after Vere's death, a letter identifies Tourneur as "in former times Secretary to Sir Francis Vere."[11]

Accepting the possibility of Tourneur's serving his soldier's apprenticeship under Vere in the Netherlands in the last years of the sixteenth century, we might well ask what the English soldiers were doing in this part of the world at this time. Illogical as it may sound, England was fighting Spain. Throughout the final years of Elizabeth's reign, a convenient rebellion was taking place in the Low Countries, a revolution which Elizabeth alternately supported and ignored, and even, at times, threatened to suppress. The Spanish control of the Netherlands was contested by the native Dutch for years before the Armada and the overt war between England and Spain. Europe's third major power, France, was also actively concerned with the fate of the Low Countries, since, clearly, a strong and uncontested Spanish domination of this area would represent an encirclement of France itself.

When English-Spanish hostilities broke out into open warfare, it was to the Netherlands that Elizabeth sent her land troops, not to Spain itself. Even in a state of declared war, Elizabeth favored the application of pressure in the safest, most indirect, and least violent ways. By forcing the Spanish to defend their holdings in the Netherlands, she diverted troops which might otherwise have been prepared to attack England. By arming the rebellious Dutch, Elizabeth saved herself the major expense and risk of an outright attack on Spain itself, on Spanish soil, and instead helped to plow a much more thoroughly prepared field. Fighting the Spanish in the Netherlands meant to Elizabeth not fighting them in Spain or England. It also meant conducting an English war with a minimal expenditure of English resources and Englishmen.

It has been said of the English campaign in the Netherlands that "a generation of English soldiers learned their trade there,"[12] and we have suggested that Tourneur was one such student. A brief look at Vere, his teacher, will tell us more about the school and the pupil.

The career of Sir Francis Vere is a simple but interesting one. He began serving his country as a soldier when he was very young, and quickly developed those qualities which we tend to associate with the best image of the military man—qualities which, probably not by coincidence, bear a striking resemblance to the hard morality revealed in Tourneur's mature dramatic works. Vere was brave. Even when commander of all English troops in the Netherlands, we consistently find him in the midst of his soldiers when danger was present. At the capture of the city of Groningen, he labored with his men in the trenches. "Twice wounded defending Sluys in 1587, he refused to retire."[13] In 1600 Vere was shot twice and had to be pulled from under his dead horse as he encouraged his soldiers at Nieuport. In 1602 he was shot close to his eye while inspecting fortifications. Vere seems never to have retreated from physical danger.

Sir Francis Vere was an independent soldier. In 1592, for example, he disobeyed direct commands in order to rescue an ally. Several times in the course of his career, he invited disapprobation from his queen for his independent thinking, yet he was so often right in his actions that the storm never broke.

The storm also never broke because Vere was a diplomat as well as a fighter. He was a successful servant of Elizabeth at The Hague, and an honest friend of The Hague in London. Negotiation between distrustful allies in a time of war is never an easy task, and many a military man has lost more glory off the battlefields than could be won on them. Vere, like the later John Churchill, helped to hold together a shaky alliance between the English and the Dutch while he excelled in fighting their common enemy.

Finally, although a diplomat, Vere was not a courtier. He had become a soldier too young to master subsequently the intricacies of Elizabethan court politics, and he wisely remained in the field and out of the court whenever he could. As a result, he never seems to have become embroiled in the domestic turmoil which ruined many another young military hero of Elizabethan England. Vere was no Essex or Raleigh.

In short, Sir Francis Vere was an intelligent, self-sufficient man, careful yet courageous, diplomatic but never sycophantic. He lived a steady and heroic life in the constant face of death. These are virtues which Tourneur clearly came to admire.

Thus, while we have virtually no direct knowledge of Tourneur's early life, family, upbringing, and education, we nevertheless can reconstruct vital formative experiences. The value of literary biography, after all, lies in the light it sheds on works of literature. A careful and measured understanding of the social and political life of late Elizabethan England, and an introduction to the Englishmen closest to Tourneur may substitute for the more conventional subject matter of biography. While it may seem a long way from Elizabethan maritime diplomacy to *The Atheist's Tragedy*, when the former is translated into human terms, the connection becomes obvious. The moral keystones of Tourneur's major literary works were forged in the complex and vital world of island Britain and her wars with Spain. The historical bravery, honesty, and independence of a Sir Francis Vere are transmuted through the prism of Tourneur's art into the themes of stoic courage and integrity which permeate the works of the mature dramatist.

IV *The London Years*

Sometime between 1600 and 1604, Tourneur gave up his career in the military and moved to London to become a professional writer. The early date of 1600 is suggested because that is the date of

The Transformed Metamorphosis, Tourneur's first published work. It would be logical to assume that this work is an initial effort by the young ex-soldier in his new vocation. On the other hand, many critics have argued that the description of the siege of Ostend in *The Atheist's Tragedy* (II. i. 28–95) suggests Tourneur may have personally been present at some portion of this engagement which began in 1601 and lasted until 1604. Since King James ended the war with Spain in 1604, it is almost certain that Tourneur was in London, writing, by the end of the first year of the new king's reign.

The bibliographical chronology of the next decade of Tourneur's life is fairly clear. In 1605, there appeared a satirical prose pamphlet presumed to be by Tourneur. *Laugh and Lie Down; Or, The World's Folly* was printed in London by Jeffrey Charlton. The attribution of the pamphlet to Tourneur is made on the basis of the initials "C. T." with which the dedication is signed. Internal evidence, such as it is, does not refute this assignment. To the extent that modern scholars and critics have noted *Laugh and Lie Down*, they agree upon Cyril Tourneur as the most likely author.

No such happy accord exists regarding the next work often assigned to Tourneur, *The Revenger's Tragedy*. Since *The Revenger's Tragedy* is the work on which the largest part of Tourneur's reputation rests, the question of attribution is a major one. Modern students of the play seem about equally divided between those who champion Tourneur's authorship, and those who line up behind another candidate, usually Thomas Middleton. This problem will be discussed in some detail in Chapter 3. In any event, *The Revenger's Tragedy* was entered on the Stationers' Register on October 14, 1607 and printed in the same year.[14] The full title page reads: "The Revenger's Tragædie. As it hath beene sundry times Acted by the King's Majesties Servants. At London Printed by G. Eld, and are to be sold at his house in Fleete-lane at the signe of the Printers-Presse. 1607." The work was first assigned to Tourneur in 1656 in the unreliable playlist of Edward Archer. It was first argued that Tourneur was not the author of *The Revenger's Tragedy* in the late nineteenth century, notably in Fleay's *A Biographical Chronicle of the English Drama, 1559–1642* (1891).

On August 28, 1609, Sir Francis Vere died, and on October 16 *A Funerall Poeme Upon the Death of the Most Worthie and True Souldier, Sir Francis Vere* appears on the Stationers' Register. This poem, signed by Tourneur, was printed before the end of the year.

The Atheist's Tragedy was entered in the Stationers' Register two years later on September 14, 1611. It was printed later in the same year with the following title page: "The Atheist's Tragedie: or The Honest Man's Revenge. As in divers places it hath often beene Acted. Written by Cyril Tourneur. At London, Printed for John Stepneth and Richard Redmer, and are to be sold at their Shops at the West end of Paules. 1611." The reference in the title to the frequent acting of the play in "divers places," as well as some presumed weaknesses, have suggested to a minority of critics an earlier date of composition and introduction upon the stage. These critics seek to prove that *The Atheist's Tragedy* antedates *The Revenger's Tragedy*, since they feel it is inferior and less sophisticated. However, even if this negative evaluation is correct—and it has been doubted, as we shall see—most modern critics have agreed with Allardyce Nicoll that "we may . . . lacking other proof, assume that *The Atheist's Tragedy* appeared on the stage about 1610 or 1611. . . . Shakespeare wrote *Cymbeline* after *Hamlet*, and Sheridan was occupied with a pantomimic entertainment after writing *The School for Scandal*."[15]

A few months later, on February 23, 1612, there was delivered to the Stationers' Company, "A play booke beinge a TrageComedye called The Noble man written by Cyrill Tourneur." *The Nobleman* has been lost but, ironically, we know more about its early stage history than about that of Tourneur's surviving dramatic works. It was probably performed at court on February 23 and again during the next Christmas season. It is possible that some incidental music composed for the court performances of this play has survived in a book of early seventeenth-century theater music.[16]

On May 24 of this same year (1612) Robert Cecil died, giving rise to Tourneur's second memorial piece, *The Character of Robert, Earl of Salisbury*. Nicoll has conclusively proven this work to be by Cyril Tourneur.

November, 1612, also saw the death of the young Prince Henry, and in December the Stationers' Register records *A Griefe on the Death of Prince Henrie*, Tourneur's third elegiac poem. Early in the next year this work, along with similar memorial poems by the dramatists John Webster and Thomas Heywood, appeared in print as *Three Elegies on the most lamented Death of Prince Henrie*.

The *Grief on the Death of Prince Henry* is the last of Tourneur's extant works. There remains one record of Tourneur as a dramatist later in this same year. On June 5, Robert Daborne (a minor dramatist) wrote to Phillip Henslowe that he had "givn Cyrill Tourneur an act of ye Arreignment of London to write."[17] The play— which has been identified with *The Bellman of London*, a dramatization of a pamphlet by Dekker—is no longer extant in any form. In terms of Tourneur's career and artistic accomplishments, this probably is no great loss. At most, Tourneur may have been responsible for preparing for the theater one act of another man's play, made from yet a third person's pamphlet.

Although *The Arraignment of London* is intrinsically unimportant, it is interesting that we learn of Tourneur's connection with the work in the way we do. While Daborne's letter reveals little or nothing about Tourneur the artist, it provides some important biographical clues which help to fill the human blanks in the preceding bibliographical chronology.

The Daborne letter enables us to make an accurate estimate of the sort of life Tourneur might have had as a dramatist. As a Renaissance playwright, he had only one market for his literary wares, the dramatic companies which would purchase outright and produce plays. If such plays were then printed, they were given to the printer either by the dramatic companies themselves, which received sole profit from the sale, or by private entrepreneurs who pirated the texts. The dramatist was paid once, before production, and the only gains he accrued through writing a successful play were those he could negotiate when selling his next work. The popular notion of the comfortable middle-class Renaissance dramatist is based solely upon the career of Shakespeare, and Shakespeare made money mostly as a capitalistic part-owner of a theatrical company, secondly as an actor, and least of all as an author.

The price paid for a new play varied from a low of perhaps five pounds to a high of around twenty.[18] An average figure might be about 10 pounds—in terms of contemporary purchasing power, the equivalent of about four hundred dollars. Clearly, a dramatist would have to write and sell several plays a year, every year, to stay solvent. Tourneur, as we have seen, was not strictly dependent upon the stage for his livelihood. He had been (and was to be again) a successful soldier. On the other hand, we have no records of Tourneur doing anything but writing between 1600 and 1613. While it is possible he wrote (*in toto* or in part) works of which no record remains, it seems clear that he was not an unusually productive artist. It is therefore more than likely that money was a constant problem, and that he lived, at least sometimes, in the precarious financial straits of many another Renaissance poet.

It is this possibility that is strongly suggested by the reference to Tourneur's hand in *The Arraignment of London*. Tourneur was "given an act" of this play to write by Robert Daborne. But Daborne himself was, in a sense, "given" the entire play to write by his employer Phillip Henslowe.[19]

Henslowe, the leading theatrical capitalist of his time, evolved a nasty and clever system of paying for plays which resulted in a flock of playwrights writing exclusively for his theaters. His system was a simple one—he kept his authors in a state of perpetual debt: "The poets received their fees from Henslowe in installments, drawing £1 or so in 'ernest' when the commission was given and as each batch of sheets was handed in, and the balance when the play was finished. This plan proved disastrous to them. The installments often found them in debtor's prison, and some of them became mere bondslaves."[20]

We know that Daborne was in debt to Henslowe when he contracted to write *Arraignment of London*. We may assume that those to whom he farmed out parts of this work were not in a much better financial condition.

When times were bad, then, Tourneur was perhaps one of a group of insolvent authors turning out hack work for Phillip Henslowe. In 1613, about a decade after he come to London to write plays, Cyril Tourneur abandoned the literary life and resumed his former career. The life of a dramatist in early Stuart England was a grim and frustrating one, and we can speculate, with regret and amusement, about the joy Tourneur must have felt at abandoning the work that was to make him, in a minor way, immortal, and turning to the work which was shortly to kill him.

V *Early Stuart Background*

The social conditions which had caused Tourneur to give up civil service in or around 1603 had changed ten years later. A brief look at this evolving environment will help us to place the second half of Tourneur's life within its proper historical context.

Tourneur's involvement with politics at this third stage of his career, was largely in the area of foreign affairs. Elizabeth died in 1603 and was succeeded by King James VI of Scotland, who became

James I and ruled until 1625. James shared Elizabeth's impulse to keep England out of war, but lacked her ability to do so. As we have seen, Elizabeth's foreign policy—which encompassed her personal life—was dictated by her understanding of her country's needs. On the other hand, "James' policy was based chiefly on personal and dynastic considerations."[21]

In 1604, James took England out of the war with Spain, and Tourneur out of business. While Elizabeth had been concerned with maintaining a balance of power between the Catholic and Protestant powers on the Continent, James believed an alliance between Catholic Spain and Protestant England could, in effect, force Europe into peace. This policy was a disastrous failure. In 1618 the Thirty Years' War broke out on the Continent, and James found himself in the rather ridiculous posture of having a significant commitment to both sides. Catholic Austria, with potent aid from Spain, attacked and overran Protestant Bohemia and the Rhenish Palatinate. The deposed monarch of these two conquered lands, Frederick, the Elector of Palatine, was a Calvinist fanatic and was married to James' daughter, Elizabeth. James reacted to one family entanglement in the chaos of European religious strife by proposing another—the infamous Spanish match between his son Charles (later, King Charles I) and the Spanish Infanta.

This scheme originated with George Villiers, earl of Buckingham, an increasingly important (and depressing) figure on the English scene in the years after 1616. Buckingham became the king's most trusted advisor during these years, not for any qualities of intellect or diplomacy, but because he cut a delightful figure at James' court: "personal favour, originating in a homosexual relationship with James, brought him supreme power."[22] As a result of this most undiplomatic liaison, Buckingham rose to become the virtual acting king of England between 1622 and 1628.

As James reached his premature dotage, and the marriage negotiations seemed bogged down, he dispatched Charles and Buckingham in person to woo the Infanta, a "romantic errand . . . as remarkable for the extraordinary complacency of the prince as for the naivete that inspired it."[23]

Fortunately, the Spanish demanded too much from the English courtiers, and Buckingham and young Charles (the former particularly) behaved boorishly in Spain. The negotiations broke down. Buckingham and Prince Charles were as childish in their reactions to the failure of their venture as they had been in their expectations, and they returned to England in October, 1623, in a violently anti-Spanish mood. Parliament met the following year, and determined to go to war with Spain. In 1625 a great expedition was organized to attack the Spanish at Cadiz, an attempt to repeat the glorious surprise attacks of the English navy in the days of Drake. Like almost every other glorious scheme of King James I, the expedition was a disaster. This particular failure, however, James was spared from witnessing, for before the expedition could depart the pathetic and senile king died. Cyril Tourneur, however, did see at firsthand the disastrous fate of this expedition, but it was the last thing he ever saw.

Tourneur's involvement with the Cadiz affair is clearly the result of his long involvement with one of the most fascinating families of the English Renaissance, the Cecils. Exactly when and where Tourneur first became entangled with the Cecil family is uncertain. Clearly Tourneur had little to do with the first great Cecil, William Cecil (the first Lord Burghley), who served as Queen Elizabeth's first minister for most of her reign. He was one of those civil servants who combined in his person great gifts of intellect, a keen sense of the practical, a willingness to work hard in even the most mundane affairs, and, most importantly, an almost instinctual sense of political survival. It has been said of William Cecil that "of all men of genius he was the most a drudge; of all men of business the most a genius."[24] William Cecil died in 1598, five years before his queen.

When he died, his places at the head of kingdom and family were taken by his son Robert, later the first earl of Salisbury. Robert had been carefully and successfully schooled in the image of his father, and, like him, was careful, rational, aloof, and well ordered. He grew into a model diplomat and statesman—realistically tough but rationally flexible. His first and most important accomplishment as a statesman was the overseeing of the peaceful succession of James Stuart upon the death of Elizabeth. For years, forward-looking Englishmen had been concerned that the absence of a clear heir to Elizabeth's crown might plunge England into a bloody civil war of disputed succession. Through the most careful, discrete, and well timed sort of negotiation, Robert Cecil averted this catastrophe. James was not unaware of his debt to Cecil, and he promised to reward Cecil for his efforts.

Robert no doubt served James with every bit as much skill and loyalty as his father had served Elizabeth. That his career was less glorious is due almost exclusively to the fact that the monarch he served was far less successful. Where Lord Burghley had led the country under Elizabeth to new and glorious heights, the earl of Salisbury devoted all his skill and attention to holding things together: Francis Bacon is reported to have told King James, speaking of Cecil, "I do think he was no fit counsellor to have made your affairs better; but yet he was fit to have kept them from growing worse."[25] All things considered, this was no mean accomplishment.

As we have already seen, Tourneur wrote a highly complimentary and dignified "Character" of Robert Cecil after his death. In this work, Tourneur reveals considerable knowledge of the Cecil family. Nevertheless, it is most doubtful that Tourneur had any personal familiarity with Robert, who was, after all, practicing first minister of England before Tourneur was twenty. Robert Cecil was not Tourneur's patron, but his cousin Edward Cecil probably was. Tourneur's "Character" of Robert is a tribute to the most prestigious and powerful member of a family, but Tourneur himself served a relatively minor limb of the Cecil tree.

Sir Edward Cecil was the third son of Thomas Cecil, himself the son of the great Lord Burghley. Although Edward was born in 1572, only nine years later than Robert, he was nevertheless a generation further removed from Elizabeth's chief minister. When he was twenty-four, in 1596, he entered the military service in the Netherlands. In 1600 he fought under Sir Francis Vere at the battle of Nieuport. In 1601 he returned to England and raised a body of one thousand soldiers to help defend Ostend, again serving under Vere.[26]

Clearly, Sir Edward Cecil and Cyril Tourneur were allied for a number of years in the same cause, in the same place. It is logical to assume that sometime during these years Cecil and Tourneur became acquainted—in the roles of commander and subordinate. Sir Edward continued his military career throughout the early years of King James' reign, while Tourneur was trying to make a career of writing in London. In about 1615 Cecil attracted the attention of Buckingham, then in the process of himself attracting increasing attention of King James.

In the early 1620s, Buckingham defended Cecil in a number of personal-political quarrels, presumably in return for the experienced soldier's guidance in military affairs. In 1625, when Buckingham took upon himself the supreme command of the ill-fated Cadiz expedition, he appointed Sir Edward Cecil as lord marshall, and general of the sea and land forces. Cyril Tourneur sailed with the Cadiz expedition as Secretary to Sir Edward Cecil.

VI *The Civil Servant*

In December, 1613, Tourneur was granted forty shillings, on the warrant of the lord chamberlain, for his work carrying letters from London to Brussels. Other records from around the same time indicate that Tourneur was frequently abroad, usually in the Low Countries. In a letter James Bathurst wrote to William Trumbull, from Nimuegen in August, 1614, we learn something of the sort of duties Tourneur was performing, as well as confirmation concerning his earlier career:

The party whose letter I enclosed to you, and whose name you could not decipher, is one Mr. Cirrill Turner, that belongs to General Cecil and was in former times Secretary to Sir Francis Vere. He told me at his first coming to this town he had been at Brussels and received many courtesies from you. He is now gone to the army with his Colonel; otherwise he had written a second letter to you that you might have better known him.[27]

This is a welcome portrait of a minor and industrious civil servant, perhaps a touch embarrassed by his exotic name.

That Tourneur was an effective agent of the crown is again testified to by the fact that at about this time, he was the recipient of an annual pension of sixty pounds from the United Provinces.

Tourneur was not always in the Low Countries, and he was not always a perfect civil servant. In the entry of September 1, 1617, in the *Acts of the Privy Council of England, 1617–18* we find "A warrant to Christopher Porter, one of the messengers of his majestie's Chamber, to bring before their Lordshipps the person of Cirell Turnor." We do not know for what offense Tourneur was arrested, but it probably was not serious, for one month later, we read in the same source of "a warrant to Acquila Weeks, Keeper of the Gatehouse, to enlarge and sett at liberty the person of Cerill Turner, upon bond taken by the clerke of the Councell attendant of Sir Edward Cicill, Knight, that the said Turner shall at all tymes be forthcomeing and make his personall appearance before their Lordships when soever he Shalbe called for."[28] Tourneur must have served Cecil well, for eight years later, as preparations were being mounted for the Cadiz expedition, he was chosen to serve as secretary to the council of war and the marshall's court under the lord marshallship of Sir Edward Cecil. On the eve of the war, he lost the first of these secretarial posts when the new king, Charles I, appointed Sir John Glanville to the position.[29]

Cecil's expedition to Cadiz departed in October, 1625. The voyage itself was uneventful. But, as many of its ships were really merchant vessels, with captains, crews, and traditions of a most unwarlike nature, the English were unable to surprise and capture the town or its shipping (in the style of Drake). Failing in the attempt to mount an outright attack, the fleet attempted to bombard nearby Fort Puntal, but again the civilian element of this comic navy suffered a failure of nerve, retreated behind the ships of the Royal Navy, and then tried to fire over them at the fort. Only when they had actually fired through the stern of a warship were they allowed to do what they had wanted in the first place—withdraw.

A landing party proceeded to attack and take the fort, which as it turned out, was not prepared to defend itself. The foot soldiers were then mustered and a march was begun to the city itself. It was discovered around midday that the orders to this army to provision itself had not gotten through. Many of the men had not eaten in twenty-four hours, and had been marching or fighting most of that time under an unseasonably hot sun.

It was determined to solve this problem by pillaging the surrounding countryside. Unfortunately, the area provided virtually no food, but vast stores of wine. This the hungry, tired, and thirsty soldiers fell upon with gusto, and the English commanders soon found themselves with a drunken army. When they tried to take away what was left of the wine, the men grew riotous. By the time the wine was gone, and the men had slept off the effects of this strange party, it was too late to attack Cadiz, now forewarned, armed, and prepared.

The fleet put to sea, hoping to intercept the Spanish treasure ships from the New World, but was as unsuccessful at this venture as it had been at everything else. Furthermore, by this time it was becoming painfully clear that the ships themselves were not adequately provisioned. Maritime equipment, ropes, and sails were rotting, and replacements had not been included. Worse, the food, which had been awful to begin with, was rapidly becoming fetid and inedible. The effects of this provisioning deficit, on top of the earlier oversight, were again disastrous. Sickness and starvation became rampant. The ships fled home toward England, losing men every day.

Unwilling to return home laden with corpses, Cecil stopped his flagship, the *Royal Anne*, at Kinsale, Ireland, to put off one hundred and sixty dying men, on December 11, 1625. Cyril Tourneur was among the abandoned, and he died on February 28, 1626.

CHAPTER 2

Early Works

TOURNEUR'S first two works, *The Transformed Metamorphosis* and *Laugh and Lie Down*, can be both revealing and misleading as introductions to the mature poet. The two works are clearly the work of a young man, experimenting with form and literary convention and discovering his subject matter. These early efforts are usually ignored by students of Tourneur and the Renaissance drama, or brushed aside as simply youthful experimentation, but such a judgment, particularly in the case of *The Transformed Metamorphosis*, is not entirely justified.

I The Transformed Metamorphosis: *The Literal Level*

This strange and trying work is difficult to summarize. In sparse outline, it is the story of a man—a poet speaking in the first person—who is lost in the darkness of depression and creative sterility. This personal darkness is the analogue of a more general absence of moral light which is debilitating the poet's society. A series of visions appears to the speaker—first visions of false hope, then a more elaborate image of an endangered island named "Delta." The poet sees a knight, Mavortio, save Delta from a beast which threatens it, and the poem ends on a note of hope.

Such a summary does not begin to do justice to a work as ambiguous, complex, dense and confusing as *The Transformed Metamorphosis*. The confusion may be a failing of the poem, but it is also in some part a necessary result of the kind of work the youthful Tourneur attempts.

This first work is a peculiar combination of obscure Renaissance satire and equally obscure allegory. The result of this blend is, of course, a very obscure Renaissance satiric allegory. Clearly, the first requisite for analysis of an allegorical work is a firm understanding of the literal action of that work. In the case of *The Transformed*

34

Metamorphosis, even the literal level is cloudy. This is largely the result of Tourneur's use of a deliberately fantastic poetic diction: the first seven-line stanza of the "Prologue" to this 609-line poem, for example, contains the words "errorie" (wandering), "Cymerianized" (dark), and "Phlegetontike" (derived from the fiery river Phlegethon of Hell, here used as an adjective to modify "sight"). The reader with sufficient patience to master this vocabulary still finds himself confronting an extremely dense and complicated plot, which shall now be examined in detail.

Tourneur begins with a "dedication" to Sir Christopher Heydon, whom he praises as "Artes Patron" (l. 5), and compares to the sun. (The sun, with related images of light and darkness, is the central image of the entire poem.) In the dedication Tourneur describes his poem in three parallel ways: ". . . this Epinyctall register,/ Rasde out by Eos rayes," "this hoarie Hiems, kill'd by Ver," and "this metamorphosde Tragoedie" (ll. 9–11). All three descriptions indicate that the poem concerns itself with the transformation of something undesirable into something good: dark into light, winter into spring, and tragedy into comedy.

There follows a message from "The Author to his Booke." Tourneur tells his poem to have no hope of becoming a great success, because it shows sin in its true colors, rather than making it attractive:

> chalke out men the way to sinne;
> Then were there hope, that multitudes wold thrust
> To buy thee.
>
> (ll. 2–4)

This is a familiar and conventional opening ploy. The "Prologue" to Jonson's *Every Man in his Humour*, for example, says that the poet will not "Purchase your delight at such a rate,/ As, for it, he himself must justly hate."[1] Webster, in his preliminary note "To the Reader" in *The White Devil*, admits that the play was unpopular, for "most of the people that come to that Playhouse, resemble those ignorant asses (who visiting Stationers shoppes their use is not to inquire for good bookes, but new bookes)."[2] Through this device the satiric author can say the times are bad and literary taste is low, and only the rare virtuous and sensitive reader will understand and appreciate the work: those who dislike the work are, of course, ignorant and evil!

Tourneur turns from addressing his book to a preliminary note "To the Reader." He says that he will try to paint honestly the world's deformity, although that deformity is now greater than any satirist could present. But he does not seek "The publike defamation of some one" (l. 19): the satire of the poem is directed at general traits of the time, not at some particular person or persons. He also notes that the poem is the product of the empty hours of some three weeks. This disavowal of specific satiric objects, and the statement of hasty composition, while perhaps true, are again highly conventional.

In the "Prologue" the poet finds himself lost in the darkness of a "black Cymerianized night" (l. 2). Who, he wonders, has "metamorphosed/ My sence?" (ll. 23–24). The entire world has been transformed into a diabolic landscape—"the azure colour'd skie,/ Is now transformed to hel's environie" (ll. 28–29). This "Prologue" is a statement of the poet's position and his concept of the world at the beginning of the poem. All is dark, the speaker sees nothing that is not tainted and hellish.

After this somewhat lengthy series of introductions (106 lines, over one-seventh of the entire work), *The Transformed Metamorphosis* proper begins. Night is taking over the heavens and turning the entire cosmos into chaos. The poet searches for a place to stand, "that I may freely view,/ Earths stage compleat with tragicke sceans of wo" (ll. 50–51). There is no mountain that will afford the poet this objective view of the world. One seven-hilled mountain is now transformed into "Hydra-headed vice" (l. 60). Nor may the poet rest in Dodon's grove (Dodona being noted for its oak trees), for help is not to be found in "a Dodonian fist" (l. 84).

The poet then prays to Jove for a resting place, and his prayer is answered: "Loe wher I stand upon a stedfast rocke" (l. 92). This rock is between the sea and the flames, and the poet moralizes, "such is the earthly state,/ Of those from earth seem to alienate" (ll. 97–98). The poet has at least risen above the earth and he may now describe what he sees.[3] He prepares himself to speak, and urges his readers ("spectators of this tragicke act," l. 106) to pay attention.

A "sacred female" (l. 113) appears, wearing the robe of Apollo and a crown of stars. This figure is derived from Rev. 12:1—"And there appeared a great wonder in heaven; a woman clothed with the sun, and the moon under her feet, and upon her head a crown of twelve stars." The sacred female might shield the poet, and might "to heav'n her minde applie" (l. 125), but the rebellious stars seek her fall, and "her robe . . ./ Is now transformed into an earthy coate,/ Of massive gold" (ll. 34–36) because she has removed her heart from heaven.

The poet sees the human race under the influence of the evening star which has been transformed into hell's torch. All are tempted to enter "blacke horrors cell," (l. 162) a trap for sinners. The poet draws the moral, "O let no wight trust to this worldly sheene" (l. 216).

Gold—the earth's "slime" and "filth" (ll. 216–21)—is the next object of Tourneur's wrath. In particular, gold cannot buy gentility (which also cannot be inherited, but shines in those that give their minds to heaven). Old age imitates youth in its craving for gold, forgetting that death is near.

We are introduced to Pan, an Arcadian shepherd (l. 254), who used to be content with his lot, but now "Pan is transform'd" (l. 254), his flock in danger of drowning, and Arcadia itself in danger of invasion by "The oceans monarch" (l. 269). As we shall see later, the Pan-Arcadia motif seems to be derived directly from Spenser's *Fairy Queen*. The poet now asks if there remains anything yet to see of the degenerate world, and at line 330 he sees the land of Delta, and the poem's chief action begins.

Delta is an idyllic and pastoral island, "environ'd with the sea,/ The hills and dales with heards are peopled" (ll. 330–31). For a long time the flocks, unafraid of anything, lived peacefully, until one day "a beast spoil'd this their sweetned rest" (l. 341). This beast, using its deceptively sweet voice, lurked in the shrubs, trapping lambs. "A gallant Knight" (l. 352) named Mavortio hears of this and arms himself to purge Delta of the beast. He is accompanied by "Truth his Page full kind,/ and by a "squire that artfull strength was call'd" (ll. 362–63). Mavortio catches the beast devouring a baby lamb, dismounts, and challenges it. The frightened beast replies that it has actually been helping Delta by chasing off wolves. Mavortio does not listen, but attacks the beast. It (variously called "he" or "she") spits poison, but Mavortio's armor repels it. The beast is wounded, but its drops of blood "transformed were to monsters" (l. 218). Nevertheless, Mavortio and his squire, now called Veramount, destroy the beast.

The poet praises Mavortio: "This noble conquest made him famouzed" (l. 449). But, although he has been nursed by the muses and by Mars, the gallant knight suffers a "sun-fall" (l. 464). Although there has been some confusion among critics about the nature of this fall, the fact that Mavortio subsequently ascends to heaven certainly seems to indicate that Tourneur means he is dead. When Mavortio does go to heaven, he takes the place of Mars, who is on earth with the muses trying to find another Mavortio. They are not successful, and find themselves lost in a "pitchy night" (l. 533). The muses, indeed, become infected, and the arts decay.

After describing this action, the poet again has a vision of darkness: "this dampy cave,/ This obscure dungeon of Cimmerian sin" (ll. 554–55). He feels his spirit begin "to rave" (l. 555). But then he pauses, and offers a word of comfort to the muses: there may yet be another Mavortio: "Your wombe may bring forth such another sonne" (l. 574). So, "hope sweet Delta hope . . . Thy Phoebus slumbereth but . . . Hee'l rise" (ll. 579–81).

The poet's vantage point is suddenly "metamorphosde to an Unicorne" (l. 583) who showers the world with brightness and purifies it. An "Eliza" appears, who will retransform the transformed and reinvigorate the "star-crown'd female" (l. 597).

Here the text proper ends, and Tourneur concludes with an "Epilogue." The darkness is drawn back to reveal the light, and the poet's spirit is brightened. We must not blame him, he says, if, when he wrote of the transformed world, his

> wittes light did waine,
> Since but with night, I could with none conferre
> In this my Epinyctall register.
>
> (ll. 26–28)

How is such a dark and obscure work to be understood? In this case, an adage from Tourneur's military milieu—divide and conquer—affords a good beginning. Allardyce Nicoll observes that "Obviously, the poem falls into two parts, the first of which, being general in theme, is comparatively easy of interpretation."[4] While Nicoll carries the division of the poem too far (speculating on different dates of composition), the basic observation is accurate. *The Transformed Metamorphosis* for all its obscurity—in one sense because of all its obscurity—is a unified poem. But this unity results from the combination of two rather different parts.

II The Transformed Metamorphosis: *Satire*

Two Elizabethan poetic conventions dominate young Tourneur's first work, allegory and satire. But these elements, although both are present throughout, are not static. Through line 330—that is, the first half of the poem—Tourneur is writing a vaguely allegorical satire. From line 330 to line 609, he presents us with a vaguely satiric allegory.

In the Renaissance, "satire" did not mean, as it seems to mean today, "parody." Rather it was a far more serious—and bleak—form of expression. The Renaissance satirist saw himself living in a deformed and deforming world, and that deformity is the subject of his poetry. According to Hallett Smith, "The significant sources of satire are not literary or philosophical; they are social and economic. For the understanding of satire, and the response to it, we need not so much an acquaintance with models and conventions, or an understanding of ideas and principles, as a knowledge of the social milieu from which the satire sprang."[5]

The subject of the first half of *The Transformed Metamorphosis* is the deformity of Tourneur's world—its people, its institutions, and even its physical structure. As Smith observes in a comment about Renaissance satire generally, "Mutability, the degeneration of man, the decay of the world and its approaching end, all cast a somber light on the activities of men."[6]

Thus, the allegorization which takes place early in the poem is social. The "seven hilled mountain" clearly refers to the seven hills of Rome, and thus, to the Roman Catholic church. "Dodon's Grove" is derived from Dodona noted for its oak groves, favored by shipbuilders and, thus, an emblem of the English Navy. Neither the decayed church nor the power of the state can lift the poet above the darkness of his world. When he does rise, as a result of an act of prayer and faith, he sees what is probably another personification of the church, the sacred female. There was a time when her robe could protect men, but now it is transformed into an earthly coat of gold—the church has become wealthy, and leads men not away from, but toward sin.[7]

Finally, lifting his allegorical personages straight out of Spenser's

Shepheard's Calendar, Tourneur laments that the shepherd Pan (the native English church) has been transformed, leaving Arcadia (England) unprotected from the Ocean's great monarch (Spain).[8]

The first half of the work, then, is a satiric look at a degenerated world, some of whose major institutions are thinly disguised by an allegorical veil. Living as Tourneur did, in an earth-centered cosmos and a human-centered earth, it is logical that this social criticism is often expressed in cosmic terms. In the Elizabethan world view, various systems in the universe are mutually interdependent.[9] A disturbed society is mirrored in a disturbed cosmos, a disturbed man. In the satiric beginning of *The Transformed Metamorphosis* the astronomical, the social, and the personal have all been plunged into a chaotic darkness.

Because the word "satiric" today has connotations of levity, it is important that we do not misjudge the bitterness and passion of Tourneur's world view in *The Transformed Metamorphosis*. Although at times the poem takes on a note of adolescent hysteria, the sincerity of the poem as personal statement cannot be dismissed. The chaotic state of the poet's "vision" is constantly emphasized— like the world around him, he is lost in darkness: "Who leades me into this concavitie?" (Prologue, l. 3); "Who hath metamorphosed/ My sence?" (Prologue, ll. 22–23); "My soule is vex'd" (l. 12); "Where shall I stand?" (l. 50 and again l. 85); "O, O, I see more than I can expresse" (l. 328); "My wittes light did waine" (Epilogue, l. 26).

Many critics have seen this quality of intense personal involvement and disgust in several of Tourneur's works. T. S. Eliot, for example, observes in Tourneur, ". . . an intense and unique and horrible vision of life . . . as might come as the result of few or slender experiences, to a highly sensitive adolescent with a gift for words."[10] What is missing from such a view of Tourneur and *The Transformed Metamorphosis* is the recognition that the poet does not stop after his satiric portrait of a fallen world—the poem has a second half.

III   The Transformed Metamorphosis: *Allegory*

It should be clear from the rather detailed outline of *The Transformed Metamorphosis* offered in section I above that the Mavortian segment of the poem differs strikingly from what has come before. The initial difference—and the logical starting point for analysis—is in the degree and kind of allegory Tourneur attempts in the second part. Until the adventures of Mavortio on Delta, Tourneur utilizes conventional allegorical characters: The sacred female is taken directly from the Bible; the seven-hilled symbol of Roman Catholicism would be familiar and obvious to a Renaissance audience; and the Pan/Arcadia references are straight out of Spenser. But "Delta" is a new allegorical land, Mavortio and his cohorts new characters. Again, in the second portion of his work Tourneur moves from description of a preexisting state of affairs ("Pan has sold his flocke," l. 296) to a description of allegorical action ("At last he ey'd/ The grisly beast as in her den she lay," ll. 365–66). What is the symbolic meaning of these characters and their actions?

Tourneur's allegory, like most, is open to multiple interpretations on multiple levels. In the case of *The Transformed Metamorphosis* the levels themselves may be more important than the interpretations. These levels include specific historical and literary analogues, as well as more general mythic and Christian readings.

Because there is a concreteness and sense of detail in the Mavortio episode which is lacking in the earlier portions of the poem, most critics have searched for a specific historical figure they believe Tourneur represented in Mavortio. There are a number of candidates, and it is useful to take a very brief look at the case which has been made for each.

What do we know of Mavortio which will help us to identify an historical analogue—if one exists? Mavortio is a soldier—his very name means "warlike." Moreover, Tourneur describes his hero with a whole series of military adjectives: "Joves martialist" (l. 506), "Heav'n upholding Atlas; warres melodie" (l. 457), and the like. But Mavortio is also an artist, fed "with pure marrow of the Muses" (l. 478), "Pieria's darling" (l. 491), and "the muses wonder" (l. 505). Is Tourneur attempting to portray a "Renaissance man," equally adept as soldier and artist? Or is he attempting to picture a soldier who makes an art of his soldiering or an artist who fights with the pen? It is interesting—though not particularly revealing—to remember that Tourneur himself practiced both crafts. The only other things we know about Mavortio are that he has defended an island ("Delta") against some sort of monster, and that he is dead.

Churton Collins in the earliest recorded analysis of *The Transformed Metamorphosis* suggests that Tourneur has attempted to portray the earl of Essex.[11] He points out that Mavortio's journey to Delta is not unlike Essex' expedition to Ireland, and that Sir Christopher Heydon, to whom the poem is dedicated, was a follower of Essex. Moreover, it has been noted that "Ireland has roughly a Delta-shape and that the Unicorn is the supporter of the Royal Arms of Scotland."[12] Unfortunately, as Nicoll pointed out in 1929, there is a difficult chronological impediment to this theory: the poem was published immediately following the downfall of Essex. Heydon was in an extremely delicate position and could hardly have welcomed a poem calling attention to his connection with the disgraced earl. Moreover, the prime mover in the action against Essex was none other than Sir Robert Cecil. It is therefore unlikely that the author of an untimely poem praising the earl of Essex could ever have reached the position of favor with the Cecil family that we know Tourneur did. In short, the date of *The Transformed Metamorphosis* is persuasive evidence that Tourneur did not intend Mavortio to represent the earl of Essex.

Nicoll does a better job of demolishing Collins' case than of building one himself. After first suggesting, then discarding Sir Christopher Heydon himself, Nicoll turns to the poetic Mavortio for his nomination: "The word Mavortio, making allowance for a common Elizabethan licence of permitting a one-letter substitution, is almost certainly an anagram of Marlowe, while the Latin form Mavortius is a complete anagram of Marlovius."[13] Nicoll's only other evidence is even more circuitous. In John Marston's *The Scourge of Vallanie* (1598), a "sprightly dread Mavortian," is ridiculed as a braggart warrior. It has been suggested that this "Mavortian" is Marlowe—or at any rate, that Marlowe appears in one disguise or another in Marston's satire. Nicoll himself is hesitant about advancing his case for Marlowe, and with good reason. While it is clearly possible that Mavortio represents a poet of some sort, the identification with Marlowe is tenuous at best. Anagrams—particularly *almost* anagrams—often prove nothing except coincidence, as witness what they have been used to "prove" about the authorship of Shakespeare's plays![14] Surely the connection with Marston's satire is more easily explained by the fact that "Mavortio" does mean "warlike," and hence is a good name for an allegorical warrior—comic or serious. Finally, it is difficult to see in Marlowe's life or writings qualities which would cause him to be depicted as a Savior figure or a mortal champion of virtue. Mavortio could be Marlowe, but we can hardly consider this identification a proven fact.

Nicoll's suggestion that Mavortio is a literary hero was pursued by

Dorothy Pym who, in 1938, suggested that the man "who, it appears to me, had the greater claim than anyone else to the pseudonym of Mavortio" was Edmund Spenser.[15] Pym's argument is based on several notable similarities between Tourneur's poem and Spenser's works. Tourneur's Pan and Arcadia are, as we have already noted, lifted straight from Spenser's *Shepheard's Calendar*. Tourneur's "Thus (pricking on the plaine) at last he ey'd/ The grisly beast" (ll. 365–66) is clearly an imitation of the first line of the *Fairy Queen*, "A Gentle knight was pricking on the plaine." Spenser's Red Cross Knight, like Mavortio, fights a dragon whose blood—like that of Tourneur's beast—turns into miniature versions of the maternal monster. Like Tourneur, Spenser mentions a Unicorn, and finally, both Tourneur's "Eliza" and Spenser's "Gloriana" are rather thinly disguised versions of Queen Elizabeth.

Clearly Pym presents valuable evidence concerning the poetic sources of Tourneur's poem. But equally clearly, this interpretation, like those discussed earlier, is not without a major stumbling block. None of this evidence suggests that Mavortio is Spenser, but rather that Mavortio resembles Spenser's *characters*. Mavortio's actions parallel those of the Red Cross Knight, but not of the creator of the Red Cross Knight. It is perhaps true that Spenser fights, in his works, the Catholic beast—but the withdrawn poet is an incongruous contrast with the glorious knight. Nor could one possibly make a case for Spenser's saving Ireland as Mavortio saves Delta. Like Nicoll, Pym advances her theory hesitantly: it "may not be an impossible one."[16] Indeed it is not, but, on the other hand, it is hardly a convincing one.

Two years later, Kenneth N. Cameron rejected Nicoll's theory that Mavortio represents a literary figure, but follows up the thought that Mavortio may be Sir Christopher Heydon. Cameron notes that "the poem is dedicated to Heydon and adorned with the Heydon crest."[17] Further, the praise offered Heydon in the dedication closely parallels the description of Mavortio in the body of the poem:

> Thou, thou that art the Muses Adonie,
> Their Pyramis, adorner of their mount,
> Thou Christalizer of their Castalie,
> Thou Lillian-rose, sprung from the horse-foote fount,
> To thee, Artes Patron. . . .
>
> (Dedication, ll. 1–5)

Mavortio is,

> Pieria's darling; cleare-streaming Helicon;
> Boetia's pearle; the nin voic'd harmony
> Heart crystalline; tongue pure Castalion;
> Delta's adamant; Elizum's melody;
> Urania's self, that sung coelestially
> Was for Mars apt, by the muses nurs'd,
> For Mars his knights, are "squires to" th muses first.

(ll. 492–98)

It is clear that both these passages attempt glorification through association—Heydon and Mavortio are allied to several mythical seats of poetry and the arts. Cameron suggests that the battle with the beast is an allegorization of Heydon's struggle with recusant Catholics at Norwich: "it seems extremely likely that Sir Christopher Heydon engaged in a campaign against them, and that Tourneur, in his eagerness to secure patronage, flatteringly exaggerated this into a national salvation."[18]

In addition to noting the striking similarity with which Tourneur praises Heydon and Mavortio, Cameron points out that in Renaissance geography, England is more closely shaped like a delta—triangular—than is Ireland. Unfortunately, Cameron bases his entire argument on an unsupported supposition: that it was "likely" that Heydon was a champion of the Protestant cause in recusant Norwich. Unless this proposition can be proved, thus supporting the interpretation of the battle with the beast, the entire case has no basis. Further, Heydon was alive and well when *The Transformed Metamorphosis* was written—but Mavortio dies. Cameron justifies this irregularity by suggesting that Tourneur was referring to Heydon's well-known astrological interests: "Heydon was so versed in astrology that he, in spirit, visited heaven."[19] This seems an extremely farfetched explanation of lines such as:

> Then Delta of her hope was quite bereaved.

(l. 510)

> Above the lofty skies, devoid of harme
> Sits Mavors spirit, as a demi-god.

(ll. 523–24)

> Before that death by life had stellified
> Great Mavors spirit in the loftie skie:
> Before his spirit in Heav'n was deified. . . .
>
> (ll. 539–41)

Cameron can hardly be said to have offered authoritative proof of the historical antecedent of Tourneur's Mavortio.

Finally, in 1948, J. D. Peter proposed one final candidate. Peter, searching for a Mavortio who would be both soldier and poet, first rejects the two Renaissance figures who most clearly fit into both categories, Sir Walter Raleigh and Sir Philip Sidney. Noting that "Eliza" in the poem may be seen as the inheritor of the virtues of Mavortio, Peter suggests that "it is quite impossible to conceive an Elizabethan poet 'flattering' the reigning Queen by informing her that she is the true heir to the virtues of one of her deceased subordinates."[20]

Mavortio, then, must be deceased royalty, and, "the obvious choice is Henry VIII."[21] Although at this point in the critical history of *The Transformed Metamorphosis* it seems queer for anyone to speak of an "obvious choice," Peter does offer some intriguing evidence. Henry was certainly seen as the defender of England against the monster of "Monasticism and Jesuitry." The poem, in flattering the father, flatters the daughter.

This interpretation, too, has its difficulties. Is Tourneur suggesting that England had been transformed into a dark and chaotic country in the reign of Henry VII, Elizabeth's grandfather? Does the reference to Eliza really suggest that this person is the "heir" of Mavortio? Upon careful investigation this reading seems dubious. Tourneur simply states: "Come, come, you wights that are transformed quite,/ Eliza will you retransforme againe" (ll. 596–97). Given the murky semantics of the poem, it seems that these lines could mean a number of things, but most likely suggest a parallel between Mavortio and the virgin queen, and not a lineal descent. Finally, Peter's thesis ignores the sense of personal immediacy the poem conveys, and advances a Mavortio who died not recently, but close to half a century before the poem appeared.

A more modern study of *The Transformed Metamorphosis* by Peter B. Murray[22] moves considerably beyond the level of literal historical allegory. Murray finds Mavortio "an embodiment of the

Phoebus-Apollo of the first half of the poem."[23] Murray makes much of Tourneur's imagery, particularly images of the sun and of lights to achieve this reading. He further extends the mythic Mavortio-Apollo into the Christian world, and discovers that "there are many indications in the poem that the myth of the sun's fall and rebirth is being used as a symbol for Christ."[24] While Murray's thesis suffers from the defect of overabstraction, his proof—frequently biblical parallels of specific passages—is convincing. Perhaps Murray's larger contribution, however, is in his suggestion that *The Transformed Metamorphosis* need not be considered solely an historical allegory, the movements of which display a one-to-one correspondence to literal fact. With Murray, criticism of Tourneur's first known work moves from looking for people to looking for patterns.

IV   The Transformed Metamorphosis: *Patterns*

The central pattern of Tourneur's poem is clearly indicated by his title: *The Transformed Metamorphosis* is about changes. Something has been changed to something else, and then is changed again. More specifically, good has been metamorphosed into evil, which is in turn transformed into good. This is the movement of the whole poem, not simply the second section. The first half of the work describes the product of the original metamorphosis; the Mavortian episode provides the catalyst and mechanism for the second change; and the conclusion of the poem—in brief counterpoint to the opening section—describes the retransformed world.

If we are correct in focusing our attention on the design of this poem, then it becomes clear why students of the poem have been unable to agree on matters of interpretation. The pattern itself can be seen as the major emphasis of the poem, rather than the specifics which can be forced—with greater and lesser success—into that system. Further, for the same reason it is not enough to simply describe the entire poem as "satire" as do C. S. Lewis and Hallett Smith. Clearly, painting a general and specific picture of a degenerated and corrupt world is part of Tourneur's plan, but it is only part. The satire and the allegory of *The Transformed Metamorphosis* are not conflicting elements, nor is this a disjointed poem. Rather, Tourneur is using satire to define a problem, allegory to suggest a solution. The pattern which emerges from these two movements—a fall followed by a rise brought about through a superhuman hero—might be called "messianic."

In his opening section, Tourneur presents in deliberately obscure language a world fallen into chaos. In the context of the Renaissance belief in corresponding levels of being, this picture is all-encompassing. The poet has lost his "vision"—he cannot find a "point of view." The one man of all men who should be a "seer" is lost in darkness. What is true on a personal level is true on a social level as well. Even "Arcadia" is subject to degeneration: its citizens and its rulers alike are subject to the corrupting influences of worldly pursuits, specifically the pursuit of gold. Finally, the universe itself is falling into darkness and chaos: the cosmic light has been extinguished. This is the problem, and Tourneur sees it with all the horror and passion of the confirmed pessimist. In his first surviving work, and throughout the rest of his writing career, he can never forget that good usually turns into evil, that brightness tarnishes and vision dims.

But Tourneur's vision is not confined to the limits of a degenerated world, regardless of the loathsome detail with which he depicts that world. Although many critics have emphasized this side of Tourneur, they neglect another, equally important aspect of this complex poet. The metamorphosis, after all, is transformed through the agency of a rejuvenating messianic force. Tourneur can at once portray a degenerate world with gruesome conviction, and in the same work, hold out hope that the filth of this world can be made beautiful.

If the general pattern of the allegory here is more important than the specific allegorical correspondences, that pattern nevertheless generates specifics. Indeed, the pattern is so broad that it encompasses and invites interpretation on several levels—personal, historical, political, mythological, and theological.

To the extent that *The Transformed Metamorphosis* is a statement of personal poetic regeneration, it seems that Cameron's thesis, noted earlier, is persuasive. There is a sense in which Mavortio is clearly related to Sir Christopher Heydon, the subject of Tourneur's "dedication." Perhaps in this context, the beast of the poem is nothing so serious as Cameron's Norwich recusancy, but something as concrete, real, petty, but vital as the perpetual wolf at the poet's door. Delta is not Britain or Ireland, but a kind of mythical land of the arts. Mavortio after all is "Pieria's darling," and "Pieria" was a mythic region of ancient Macedonia in which the muses were worshipped. In this most limited sense, the poem may well be a state-

ment by a young poet who had just recently left the security of
military service, to the effect that he is in desperate need of an
"Artes Patron." Such a patron would accordingly be a very real, if
somewhat worldly, messiah to someone in Tourneur's position.
But there is a larger sense in which *The Transformed Metamorphosis* is a statement of personal despair and regeneration. Clearly
the persona of the poem is searching for something more than patronage. As poet, and as man, he is lost in a "Cymerianized night"
but, during the course of the poem, comes into the light. This
particular transformation, however, does not seem to take place
through the agency of Mavortio, but earlier in the poem (ll. 90–98).
The poet has already rejected (or been rejected by) the "seav'n hill'd
head" and "Dodon's grove" (as noted above, standard symbols for
Roman Catholicism and the British Navy). The poet is rejecting
both spiritual and military or worldly power: neither will provide
the vantage point from which he can see and understand the world
about him. He turns to faith:

> Where shall I stand? O heav'n conduct me now,
> Jove Israellize my tongue, and let my voyce
> Prevayle with thee; shew me the manner how
> To free me from this change: O soule rejoyce,
> For heav'n hath free'd me from black hels annoies.
> O see, O see, jove sets me free from thrall,
> Such is his love to them that on him call.
> Loe where I stand upon a stedfast rocke,
> Whose peerelesse trust is free from all compare . . .
>   such is the earthly state,
> Of those from earth seeke them to alienate.
>   (ll. 85–93, 97–98)

If this is simple theology, it is nevertheless good pragmatic advice
for a beginning poet: the way to avoid worldly entanglements is
simply to avoid the world. Spiritual and military power, and the
entire range of worldly temptations they symbolize, are blinding
and imprisoning. If the poet and the man is to see clearly the world
around him, he must base his vision on a foundation of faith—a faith
which Tourneur describes as a solid and "stedfast rocke" (note the
echo of Christ's charge to St. Peter in the rock-faith image). The
poet must disengage himself from the world in order to engage

himself in it poetically. The man must rise above his surroundings on the rock of faith if he is to understand himself and where he is.

Within the historical context, the allegorical pattern of *The Transformed Metamorphosis* seems relevant to a number of figures, both military and artistic. Mavortio, in a rough way, resembles many actual figures of Tourneur's time, and Tourneur seems to encourage several such identifications. Tourneur creates an archetype, and then suggests, through a number of poetic devices, specific individuals who partially fulfill the archetypal pattern. Thus, for example, the poem, as Pym suggests, is filled with situations, characters, and actual lines from the works of Spenser; perhaps Tourneur does not mean for us to identify Mavortio as Spenser, but to be reminded of some of the battles Spenser fought through his characters.

Possibly there is also something Mavortian in Sir Francis Vere, a military hero particularly close to Tourneur, who, like Spenser, fought Catholicism. Again Mavortio is inspired by the same ideal of the complete courtier—poet and soldier—that inspired the lives of actual men like Raleigh and Sidney. In short, Tourneur creates in Mavortio an ideal, to which all sorts of historically real personages probably contributed. Trying to identify the solid and specific historical analogue to Mavortio may be like trying to discover the hero of a telephone directory.

Politically, the typological pattern of *The Transformed Metamorphosis* is clearer. Any poem dated 1600 in which there appears a character named "Eliza" can be assumed to refer to Queen Elizabeth. It is somewhat more difficult to determine what precise role the virgin queen plays in Tourneur's work. The unicorn which is transformed into "Eliza" at the conclusion of the poem has little apparent connection to the preceding Mavortio episode. Perhaps the connection was too clear to need to be made. Elizabeth had surely fought the Catholic beast with notable success during her reign, whether that beast had manifested itself in the Armada, the Netherlands, or Mary. Moreover, like Mavortio, Elizabeth arrived on the scene at just the right time. As the Arcadian peace of Delta was threatened by the arrival of the beast "that Deltaes damage sought" (l. 343), so the Tudor serenity wrought out of the chaos of the Wars of the Roses was threatened by Elizabeth's sister Mary. As Mavortio arrived to restore peace, so did Elizabeth. At any rate, it is clear that Tourneur wished to associate his queen with the Mavor-

tian, messianic pattern: "Eliza will you retransforme againe"
(ll. 598).

The fact that Tourneur wanted to associate the pattern of his
poem with the life of his queen does nothing to weaken the argument of those who, like J. D. Peter, see in that poem a resemblance
between Mavortio and Elizabeth's father, Henry VIII. As Peter
notes, the royal saviour, soldier, and poet is a recognizable type of
Henry; there is no reason to disassociate him from the poem.
Equally, those who see in Tourneur's unicorn a reference to the
royal arms of Scotland, and hence, to the then king of Scotland,
James VI, probable successor to the ailing Elizabeth's throne, may
well be right. Tourneur might conceivably have been working into
his poem the first Stuart as well as two Tudors. Mavortio is a model
of what a late Elizabethan might call an ideal monarch. He combines
the strength of a knight with the education of a poet—he is equally
the child of Mars and of the Muses, equally the master of words and
of swords. It was not at all uncommon for an Englishman of 1600 to
say that of this pattern Henry VIII was, Elizabeth is, and God
willing, James would be.

Tourneur, in effect, creates a mold into which he can inject aspects of important historical and political figures of his time. The
identification of Mavortio with any of these figures is of necessity
loose. In some cases, we base such identification on very tenuous
literary relations (for example, Marlowe). In others, the evidence of
the poem seems conclusive (for example, Elizabeth). Tourneur is
dealing with an archetype which fits, at times, certain aspects of
several actual people.

This pattern fits much more specifically into a mythic rather than
historic framework. As Murray notes, the Mavortio episode when
coupled with the major imagery of the poem, is a relatively simple
working out of the common mythic theme of cyclical rejuvenation.[25]

Beginning with the seasonal rejuvenation of the earth's fertility,
similar rejuvenation myths have developed in a number of cultures
throughout the world. Often such myths develop a "green man"
figure, a god who, representing fertility, dies, and then, with the
earth, returns to life in the spring. Many critics, such as Northrop
Frye, believe that this myth survives in complex and sophisticated
form in much of literature. Since the rejuvenating god of fertility is
often symbolized or embodied in the sun—as is Mavortio ("Thy
Phoebus slumbereth but in Thetis lap," l. 580)—it is not unreason-

able to suggest that Tourneur's messianic type is another version of the mythic pattern of death and rejuvenation—metamorphosis and transformation.

Of course, the most familiar version of the seasonal rejuvenation myth in Western culture is the Christian myth. Christ is clearly a version of the mythic fertility god. Indeed, some Christians see in the universality of the seasonal myth foreshadowings of the coming of Christ.[26] There can be no doubt that, whatever else he is, Mavortio is a type of Christ, the ultimate Christian soldier. He brings light to a dark world; he comes to save the Deltan sheep from temptations of the beast, and ascends into heaven, where he is welcomed by Jove, next to whom he takes his seat. But although gone, Mavortio will return:

> O heav'ns! O sweet heav'n fed Muses stay.
> Exclaime not on the sacred heav'ns for this:
> But as a mother (that her childe doth misse)
> Lament: and be your heart from despair wonne:
> Your wombe may bring forth such another sonne.
>
> (ll. 570–74)

Although the pattern of the messianic rejuvenator of the world may be buried in the universal human subconscious, there is no question as to how that pattern manifested itself to Tourneur and his contemporaries. The hero of a poem who was nurtured by heaven, who brought light to a dark world, ascended to the right hand of God, and promised to return could only be, in one form or another, Christ. *The Transformed Metamorphosis* is a poem about a pattern—chaos restored to order—into which, Tourneur intimates, a number of actual figures including the poet himself fit. The pattern itself, the skein into which are woven these historical threads, is generally mythic and specifically Christian.

V Laugh and Lie Down

Tourneur's other early nondramatic work, *Laugh and Lie Down, or The World's Folly* is *The Transformed Metamorphosis* without the second "transformation." It is a stock and undistinguished portrait of the fallen world.[27] Tourneur's satire takes the form of a very simple allegorical dream vision. The poet is on an island, with one major city (England and London, one presumes), before a large house. This house, it turns out, is the "Fort of Folly"—something of a cross between a lunatic asylum and a workhouse for the foolish. The poet is given a tour of the fort, during which he meets and observes all manner of fools—fops, whores, lovers, gluttons, gallants, country bumpkins, and the like. Many of the inmates of the fort, for some unspecified reason, occupy themselves by describing their condition, and then singing a more or less appropriate ballad: for example, "a man of some wealth: but, with entering into suretie, and taking up Creditte, and giving interest, fell so farre to decay, by leaving his Trade to his Servauntes charte . . ." now sings "the Ballad of Whilom I was, To the tune of Tom Tinker" (ll. 187–98).

At the very end of the poem, the poet reveals for the first time that all this is a dream: "So that I never heard more of any of them, but was ever man so troubled in his sleepe?" (ll. 826–27).

Clearly, *Laugh and Lie Down* is not a first rate work of art. Its plot, which consists strictly of a walk through an allegorical house, is lethargic; its characters lack both the individuality and the satiric bite which can invigorate allegorical personifications; its theme—that there is much that is foolish in the world—while true, is trite and commonplace. Nevertheless, the poem is not without interest in the study of Tourneur's career, first, as a satirical vision, and second, as a predramatic work.

As a work of satire, it is curious to note how *Laugh and Lie Down*, a very plain pamphlet intended for a strictly popular audience, is nevertheless clearly related to "high" and even esoteric art forms. It represents a popularizing trend of the Renaissance not without significance in the history of ideas and art. Although it would be oversimplification to claim a direct source-product relationship, one can see plainly in Tourneur's popular pamphlet the influence of Chaucer, Spenser, and perhaps even Dante.

Although Chaucer did not invent the allegorical dream vision, he is certainly responsible for bringing that form into the mainstream of English literary types. *Laugh and Lie Down* would not have been possible without *The Parliament of Fowls*, *The House of Fame*, and *The Book of the Duchess*. In each of these works the poet visits, in a dream, a world of allegorical abstractions, frequently like Tourneur's Fort of Folly, housed within a specific edifice. Often Chaucer's dream visions, like Tourneur's, aim at "a certain amount of political or social satire."[28] Tourneur is clearly not writing a work comparable to *The Parliament of Fowls*, but he is writing in a tradition which is directly descended—both in terms of chronology and of quality—from Chaucer.

While Chaucer's dream visions were not without satirical content, it was Spenser who developed the set piece of the allegorical "place" in which are revealed the variations of a particular vice. We have already seen the Spenserian influence on Tourneur in *The Transformed Metamorphosis*. Indeed, the Fort of Folly is obviously related to the brief picture in Tourneur's earlier work, of the Palace of Lust:

> a shining hal,
> Bedeckt with flowers of the fairest hew . . .
> This little roome, will scarce two wights containe,
> T'enjoy their joy, and there in pleasure raigne. . . .
> But next thereto adjoynes a spacious roome,
> More fairly farre adorned than the other. . . .
> The dradfull floore of this deceitfull place,
> Is all of quagmires, to intrap the wight
> That treades thereon: yet cover'd o're with grasse
> Of youthful hew, al pleasing to earth's sight,
> So doth satan worke his div'lish spight.
>
> (ll. 190–208)

Spenser's *The Fairy Queen* contains a number of these allegorical halls of evil, perhaps most notably Acrasia's Bower of Bliss. What Spenser's portraits and Tourneur's have in common is that they permit the poet to discuss at some length and under one allegorical roof the varieties of a particular vice or temptation and their relationship to each other.

Finally, there are several ways in which *Laugh and Lie Down* seems at least superficially to imitate Dante's *Divine Comedy*, particularly the "Inferno" and "Purgatorio" sections. Like Dante's persona, Tourneur's protagonist has a guide through his allegorical world—a henpecked husband: "brought in by my guide, (the poore man, that was in miserable taking with a woman, I will not say his wife:) there he tooke me by the hand, and setting down by me, willed me to be silent, and onely give eare to the discourses that I should heere betwixt two fooles . . ." (ll. 528–32).

Like the *Divine Comedy*, *Laugh and Lie Down* groups various classes of sinners in an appropriate place: "But at the entrance to the

first base Court, wher/ walking of Horses was the chiefest exercise of
Idle people . . ." (ll. 28–29). Thus, like Dante, Tourneur—at least
at times—seems to be creating both a satiric microcosm of a fallen
world, and a place in which fools are being punished for their folly,
after the fact. Many of the inhabitants are not at the time of the
narration being foolish, but being punished for their previous folly:

> . . . he led me into a large Roome, paved with rough flint stone, in the
> midst whereof, was a kinde of standing water, that, (when it was stirred)
> gave a kind of sent that would have kilde a horse: Alasse (quoth I) Father,
> what shall I doe heere? Why (quoth he) you must know, that they have
> spent their wealth in perfumes, sweete waters, and delicate Odors, must
> first heere have patience with a little unpleasing savour. . . . (ll. 113–19)

These punishments parallel those of the *Inferno* and *Purgatorio* in
that they are extensions of—and hence, appropriate to—the original
crime for which they are being exacted.

Finally, Tourneur reminds us of Dante through the device of
identifying the Fort of Folly as a kind of Hell or Purgatory: "O
Heavens, what a Hell is this?" (ll. 173–74); "This is a Pur-
gatorye . . . " (ll. 341–42); "Wel I was exceedinge glad when I was
awake, I was so well and safely delivered out of this Purgatory"
(ll. 827–28). Indeed, there are some eleven overt references to the
Fort of Folly as Purgatory as well as several references to hell and
devils.

In spite of these otherworldly references, Tourneur's pamphlet
remains a satiric description of the world in which the poet lives.
For example, among his fools Tourneur notes several honest
men—men who would not be punished in the afterlife, but would
be regarded as fools in the real world. The Fort of Folly includes a
lawyer who "had too much care of conscience, for his worldly com-
moditie" (ll. 678–79); a usurer who forgives debts and pities widows,
orphans, and the poor; and a banker who has determined he would
"rather to die a poore Christian, than to live a rich Jew" (l. 721).
These characters are foolish because they profess and practice honesty in a dishonest world. Tourneur, then, is not depicting hell but a
hellish world in which folly abounds, and most, but not all, fools are
evil. Although this vision is not particularly well presented in *Laugh
and Lie Down*, it does seem to raise Tourneur's work a notch above
many of the railing satiric pamphlets of his time. It is a vision of man

and his world which we have already seen in *The Transformed Metamorphosis* and will see again in Tourneur's dramatic works. There are other ways in which *Laugh and Lie Down* is a precursor to Tourneur's plays. Most simply, he is aiming this work at the same audience that might frequent the popular Renaissance stage. This poem is not aimed at the aristocracy (there are few aristocratic species of folly depicted in it), nor is it a work for the totally unlettered (who could not read it), nor the totally impoverished (who would not have the time to be interested in it). Rather it is directed straight toward the city bourgeoisie—shopkeepers, apprentices, well-to-do merchants and their wives—who also comprised the audience at the Globe and other Elizabethan theaters.

Tourneur's potential audience for *Laugh and Lie Down* no doubt helps to explain the heavy amount of ballad material in the work. Ballads were, like plays and pamphlets, a popular entertainment. Indeed, many of the ballads Tourneur mentions in his pamphlet also appear in the dramas of the day, especially in the plays of Shakespeare. In fact, so many of the ballads in the poem are mentioned or sung in Shakespeare's plays that it is difficult not to infer a connection.[29] Of the twenty-four ballads and tunes mentioned in *Laugh and Lie Down*, five, or better than one in five, appear in Shakespeare's plays; for example, "All a greene Willowe" (l. 294) is sung by Desdemona in *Othello* and "The Three merry men" (l. 657) is a tune used in *Twelfth Night*. This suggests, although it certainly does not prove, that Tourneur may have been paying some careful attention to Shakespeare's plays as early as 1605, before he himself attempted to write for the stage.

There are other hints that Tourneur's attention may have been shifting to the dramatic mode as he was writing *Laugh and Lie Down*. The poet is awakened at the end of the poem by a dramatic masque beginning in the Fort of Folly. At the start of the work, in his address "To the Reader," he comments, concerning the piece, that "there are changes in it enough to make a Play." That this self-evaluation is not true renders it nonetheless interesting as a clue to its author's frame of mind.

Finally, and perhaps most importantly, *Laugh and Lie Down* seems predramatic from the standpoint of narrative form. The greater portion of the piece is written as dialogue. In this work, unlike *The Transformed Metamorphosis*, Tourneur allows his characters to reveal and define themselves by what they say, not by what the narrator says about them. Here is a random illustration of almost purely dramatic dialogue in which the poet is conversing with the porter of the Fort of Folly. The porter speaks of Folly herself:

. . . she is a kinde woman, and will give you countenaunce whensoever you come: for shee loves Straungers esceedinglye, and entertaineth them most kindely. Alas (quoth I) these wordes of yours are straunge, I know not what to make of them: I am not for hir hand, except she have neede of me in some better service, then yet I heere of.

Why (quoth he) let me tell you, it were straunge, that you should spend your wits, with your wealth . . . I will warrant you pleas'd for your paine.

No (quoth I) imaginations of ydlenesse are but losse of time. . . . (ll. 91–101)

This is embarrassingly awkward dialogue, but it is dialogue, and hence, dramatic. In *Laugh and Lie Down* Tourneur moves from the omnipotent narrative voice toward a form of multiple points of view—he is moving toward the theater.

CHAPTER 3

The Revenger's Tragedy:
Authorship

I T is ironic that the authorship of *The Revenger's Tragedy*—the real foundation of Tourneur's lasting reputation—is open to serious question. Ironic or not, one cannot discuss the art of this play without first dealing with the serious and complex questions which surround doubtful attribution. Fortunately, a survey of these questions is not the exercise in dry bibliographical or textual analysis it threatens to be. Indeed, the careful study of the authorship of *The Revenger's Tragedy* is almost a drama in its own right—a tragicomedy perhaps.

Since some knowledge of the play itself is a prerequisite to understanding the problems of establishing authorship, it is necessary to begin with a brief outline of the plot of this perennially fascinating work.

I *Plot*

Compared to other plays of its type, *The Revenger's Tragedy* does not have a particularly complex plot. But like other Jacobean revenge tragedy, it is characterized by rather elaborate patterns of action. The action is set in an unnamed Italian court, ruled by a corrupt and sensualistic Duke and his second wife, the Duchess, equally lustful and corrupt. Each has children by a previous marriage—the Duke, two sons (Lussurioso and Spurio—a bastard), the Duchess, three (Ambitioso, Supervacuo, and an unnamed "Youngest Son"). As the play begins, Vindice, a discontented scholar, watches and comments upon a procession of the royal family. The Duke he describes as a "royall letcher," Lussurioso "as impious steept as hee," Spurio, "true-begott in evill," and the Duchess "Will doe with the Divill" (I. i. 1–4). Vindice reveals to the audience the skull of his "poysoned love" (17), Gloriana, who has been murdered by the Duke for rejecting his lecherous advances. Vindice, joined by

57

his brother Hippolito, their mother Gratiana, and sister Castiza, reveals further that his father had been disgraced by the same Duke and as a consequence "dyed of discontent" (142–43). Vindice thus has two reasons to "give Revenge her due" (117). Hippolito tells Vindice that Lussurioso is looking for some unscrupulous man to serve as his pander, and Vindice, seeing an opportunity for revenge, undertakes to disguise himself and "turne into" (153) just such a "man a'th time" (102). This entire exposition takes place within a 153-line scene, which, in addition to setting into motion a complex series of events, is theatrically powerful and poetically compelling. It is a masterful opening scene.

We soon see at first hand the decayed core of the court. The Duchess' "Youngest Son" is sentenced to death by the Duke for the rape of the wife of an old lord, Antonio, and the Duchess vows to revenge herself by seducing her stepson Spurio. To avenge his mistreatment as a bastard, Spurio agrees to be seduced, "for indeed a bastard by nature should make Cuckolds,/ Because he is the sonne of a Cuckold-maker" (I. ii. 223–24).

Vindice, disguised as "Piato," is hired by Lussurioso to pander to his own sister. Although appalled, he resolves to "try the fayth" (I. iii. 199) of Castiza, since "Another might have had the same office" (200). Castiza rejects the offer of her disguised brother, but Gratiana is converted and also attempts unsuccessfully to tempt her daughter. Upon his return Vindice tells Lussurioso of the affair between Spurio and the Duchess, and Lussurioso, attempting to catch the incestuous pair making love, bursts into his stepmother's bedchamber, sword in hand. Instead of Spurio, he finds the Duke, and is promptly arrested for attempted assassination. His stepbrothers, while pretending to plead for Lussurioso, actually urge the Duke to condemn him: "We know the trespasse is unpardonable" (II. ii. 287). The Duke, who plans to pardon Lussurioso, sees through Supervacuo and Ambitioso, but pretends to agree with them, and gives them his ring so that they might have Lussurioso executed. Lussurioso, however, is quickly pardoned and freed, and when Supervacuo and Ambitioso deliver their "command of present death . . . Unto our brother, the Dukes sonne" (III. iii. 2–3), their own natural brother, still jailed for his rape, is mistakenly executed. The brothers learn of this error with the simultaneous appearance of the unharmed Lussurioso and the severed head of the Youngest Son.

Vindice, meanwhile, has been commissioned by the Duke to find him a mistress, but instead, he lures the Duke to a dark and out of the way corner, and presents to him, in the dark, the poisoned lips of the skull of the dead Gloriana, in a grotesquely appropriate act of revenge. As the Duke is dying, Spurio and the Duchess arrive meet, and begin to make love. The hidden Vindice and his brother force the Duke to die watching.

Lussurioso, angry with "Piato" for misleading him into breaking into the Duke's bedchamber, asks Hippolito to procure for him another malcontent to kill "Piato." Naturally, Hippolito fetches Vindice again, who is promptly hired to kill himself. First, however, Vindice and Hippolito confront their mother and accuse her of aiding in the seduction of Castiza. Gratiana, when apprised of Vindice's role in the affair, admits her error and repents. Vindice and Hippolito then disguise the dead body of the Duke in "Piato's" clothing and tell Lussurioso it is Piato. He discovers, however, that it is his father, and assumes that "Piato" has killed him and exchanged clothes. Lussurioso becomes Duke. During a masque celebrating his ascension, Vindice and Hippolito and other discontented lords disguise themselves as masquers and "steale out their swords and . . . kill the foure at the table . . ." (V. iii. s.d.56), including Lussurioso. Spurio, Ambitioso, and Supervacuo, also planning to kill the new Duke during these revels, arrive. Discovering their victim is already dead, they quarrel with each other over who is the successor, and each mortally wounds the other. Since all heirs to the dukedom are dead, old Antonio becomes duke. He wonders how the old Duke died, and Vindice proudly claims the deed. Antonio, noting that "you that would murder him would murder me" (V. iii. 148), orders Vindice and his brother led off "to speedy execution" (145) as the play ends.

II *Bibliographic Facts*

In Renaissance England, as noted earlier, plays were considered more as theatrical raw material than literary art. As a consequence, *The Revenger's Tragedy*, like so many of its brothers, came into the world without an acknowledged parent. A printer, George Eld, was the godfather, entering the play in the Stationers' Register on October 7, 1607. The entry, making no mention of authorship, reads in full: "Twoo plaies th one called *the revengers tragedie* the other, *A trick to catch the old one.*" Although neither play is assigned an

author, *A Trick to Catch the Old One* has subsequently been assigned with some certainty to Thomas Middleton, a fact of interest
to those who argue for Middleton's authorship of *The Revenger's
Tragedy.* Unfortunately, there are not enough double entries in the
Register during this period to enable anyone to say for sure what
such entries mean. They could imply shared authorship, or merely
that the owner of two unrelated manuscripts happened to bring both
to the Stationers' company for entry simultaneously. The dual entry
with *A Trick to Catch the Old One* may be an important clue to the
authorship of *The Revenger's Tragedy,* or it may simply mark
George Eld's efficiency.

Another place to look for authorship of a Renaissance play, of
course, is on the title page of the printed work itself. Title-page
information is useful, although by no means infallible: witness the
many plays assigned to Shakespeare by printers eager to capitalize
on a name with guaranteed drawing power. The title page of this
work reads, in full,

THE/ REVENGERS/ TRAGEDIE./ *As it hath beene sundry times Acted,/ by the
Kings Maiesties/ Servants./* AT LONDON/ Printed by G. ELD, and are to be
sold at his/ house in Fleete-lane at the signe at the/ Printers-Presse./ 1607.

(Another edition, with only the date changed, was issued in 1608.)
The only useful bit of information regarding authorship which can
be deduced from this title page concerns its stage history. Title-page
accuracy is generally reliable in matters of theatrical production,
since the buying public would more likely be aware of such theatrical data than of the author's name. Those who contend that Tourneur wrote this play have pointed out that Middleton was not known
to have had anything to do with the Kings' Men at this time, indeed,
that he was employed during this period by a rival theatrical company.

Stationers' Register and title-page information about authorship
may be called "external evidence": evidence based upon some objective authority outside the play itself, which is presumably knowl-
edgeable, reliable, and contemporary. Neither of the two principal
bits of external data concerning *The Revenger's Tragedy,* unfortunately, proves authorship. In fact, in a pattern we shall see repeated
and repeated—until it becomes a leitmotiv of this chapter—one

piece of evidence seems to point to Tourneur, another to Thomas Middleton.

Perhaps the best sort of external evidence for the authorship of a particular work is the mentioning of that work, coupled with an author, by a contemporary observer (for example, Mere's list of early Shakespeare plays in *Paladis Tamia*). But *The Revenger's Tragedy* did not merit mention in this way for almost half a century. The first recorded attribution of the play takes place in 1656 in a list of plays compiled by Edward Archer. Archer says that the author is "Tournour." In a similar list, based upon Archer's, but correcting some misattributions, Francis Kirkman adds the Christian name "Cyrill."[1]

What sort of evidence are these seventeenth-century playlists? We simply do not know. Clearly Archer and Kirkman are not contemporaries of Tourneur (or Middleton), but equally clearly they are much closer than we are. Certainly, forty-nine years after the performance and publication of *The Revenger's Tragedy* there would be some men living who remembered the initial appearance of the play. On the other hand, these playlists, particularly Archer's, are notoriously inaccurate: Middleton's *A Trick to Catch the Old One*, for example, is badly listed by Archer as Shakespeare's. Kirkman was more accurate than Archer (for example, he correctly attributes *A Trick to Catch the Old One* to Middleton) but still hardly a model of scholarly precision. It may well be, as several Middletonians have suggested, that Archer simply assigned *The Revenger's Tragedy* on the basis of similarity of title to *The Atheist's Tragedy*, a known Tourneur piece. On the other hand, it is rare for Archer and Kirkman to misattribute in the direction of obscurity: in most cases where they are wrong, they give an obscure author's work to a more famous contemporary. Tourneur, in 1656, was obscure—Middleton was not. A balanced view of the Archer and Kirkman attributions suggests that they constitute a bit of weak and by no means conclusive evidence in support of Tourneur.

If one is to call the early playlists "external evidence," then three sources of external data concerning *The Revenger's Tragedy* are notable for their inconclusiveness. The title page points indirectly at Tourneur; the Stationers' Register points indirectly at Middleton; and the playlists point directly—but weakly—to Tourneur again. For the next two centuries Archer's attribution would rest. But, like a time bomb ticking away just under the surface of the ground, the weakness of that attribution was about to be exploded.

III *Early Doubts*

In the late nineteenth and early twentieth centuries, attribution studies enjoyed a brief vogue. Perhaps in part because this was the period in which the study of the modern languages was fighting for scholarly and academic recognition, the methods—or rather, the methodological terminology—of the sciences plays an important role in what has been called the "golden age" of attribution.[2] Any Elizabethan play about which the slightest doubt of authorship could be offered was fair game for the attributors: indeed, a great many plays about which there were no legitimate doubts of authorship also became grist for the attribution mill. Thus, on the one hand, we find assignments of anonymous plays to authors for whom no other extant dramatic works are available for comparison, and on the other, the disintegration of the Shakespeare canon. Any passage—or play—which seemed to the critic unworthy of the Bard of Avon could be attributed to some other, lesser, dramatist. And here, in fact, was the great flaw of these studies. Far too frequently, "scientific" attribution studies were simply critical impressionism masquerading in the guise of the objective pursuit of truth.

Given the real and important differences between *The Revenger's Tragedy* and *The Atheist's Tragedy*, and the doubtful circumstances surrounding the assignment of authorship of the earlier play, we need not be surprised to find Tourneur's claim to authorship challenged during this period. Several critics felt that the case for Tourneur was weak, but many were not prepared to offer an alternate candidate. Felix Schelling's discussion of the issue in his *Elizabethan Drama* is an example of these early doubts:

Concensus of opinion assigns this play to Tourneur although his name appears on neither of the contemporary quartos. It must be confessed that neither the style nor the characterization of *The Revenger's Tragedy* resembles that of *The Atheist's Tragedy*, above which the former rises as far aesthetically for the living realism of its effects, its mastery of horror, and its passages of poetic power, as it falls below the well-defined moral intent of the earlier play.[3]

Perhaps the first of these turn-of-the-century critics to seriously propose an alternative author for the play was F. G. Fleay in 1891:

The Revenger's Tragedy was acted by the King's Servants. It was entered S. R. [*sic*] along with Middleton's *Trick to Catch the Old One*. Elde also published *Northward Ho*, by Dekker and Webster, to the latter of whom I should have attributed *The Revenger's Tragedy*, were it not for the universal concensus of the authorities, founded on some evidence unknown to me. The play was published anonymously, and seems to me far superior to anything Turner (judging from his known writings) could have produced.

Fleay seems so pleased with his sarcastic aside about other critical authorities that he repeats it eight pages later in his discussion of Webster: "The extreme likeness of this play [*The White Devil*] to *The Revenger's Tragedy* (attributed by common consent to Tourneur, on I know not what authority) is remarkable." Considering the rather positive tones of these assertions, Fleay offers little hard evidence for his attribution: he notes certain similarities of plot (poisonings and discoveries—which are an extremely common convention of the Elizabethan revenge play, witness *Hamlet*) and an undefined "Websterian" meter.[4]

It is also during this period of early doubts concerning Tourneur's authorship of *The Revenger's Tragedy* that Thomas Middleton is first proposed as the play's author, appropriately enough by his champion for the next quarter of a century, E. H. C. Oliphant. As early as 1910, Oliphant was considering Middleton, but stops just short of a positive nomination of his candidate. After first noting that he "cannot conceive" of the same man writing *The Revenger's Tragedy* and *The Atheist's Tragedy*, Oliphant confesses, ". . . but I know of no one among the named writers of the time to whom I would attribute it, unless it be Middleton, to whose verse alone the swing of the verse of *The Revenger's Tragedy* makes some approximation." After suggesting that a careful study of the internal evidence will justify such a hunch—a suggestion he himself takes some sixteen years later—Oliphant concludes: "I prefer, however, to consider *The Revenger's Tragedy* as the greatest work of its period of that prolific writer 'Anon,' and look upon the establishment of the identity of the author as one of the chief problems to be tackled by the students of Elizabethan drama."[5]

In this period of doubt, Tourneur was not without his defenders. H. Dugdale Sykes notes internal resemblances between *The Atheist's Tragedy* and *The Revenger's Tragedy* in their use of "numerous . . . contractions," "rhymed antithetical couplets," "the brother-another rime," and the phrases "serious business" and "'Tis

oracle." As Sykes himself notes, his internal comparison was based "perhaps unwisely" on a very bad text, which renders his major points highly dubious: it is unlikely that authorship can be proved by editorial handling of contractions after the playwright's death. Notwithstanding this admission, Sykes speaks with a tone of absolute confidence depressingly familiar in the history of this controversy: "In this I venture to think that I have been successful, having discovered sufficient internal evidence to justify the traditional ascription of *The Revenger's Tragedy* to the author of *The Atheist's Tragedy.*"[6]

From about 1890 to 1925, then, there was much doubt that Cyril Tourneur wrote *The Revenger's Tragedy.* More than one alternate candidate was proposed. All that was lacking was evidence.

IV   *Comparisons and Controversy*

In the next decade (1925–1935) the argument stabilized and solidified. Those who did not believe the play to be Tourneur's settled upon Middleton as an alternate author and began to amass a substantial body of internal evidence to support their claimant. The backers of Tourneur adopted a somewhat defensive posture. They did not seek new evidence backing their candidate, but reaffirmed the value of the older external evidence of the playlists, plus some rather impressionistic opinions concerning supposed similarities between *The Revenger's Tragedy* and *The Atheist's Tragedy.* Since the Middletonians tend to begin their arguments with an equally impressionistic feeling of dissimilarity between the two plays, the controversy of this period at times takes on a circular appearance.

In 1926 Oliphant, whom we have already seen tentatively advancing the case for Middleton, reaffirms his position much more vigorously. He presents the first hard evidence in support of the Middleton candidacy. Oliphant begins by asserting the expected dissimilarity between *The Revenger's Tragedy* and *The Atheist's Tragedy:* "They are so utterly unlike, so markedly at variance in conception of prosodic law, that it is nothing less than amazing that Tourneur's authorship of the greater of the two plays has been so little questioned. As I have said, the verse is not the verse of Tourneur. . . . Nor do the two plays yield much in the way of parallel passages." He proceeds, at some length, to argue that *The Revenger's Tragedy* has

almost all the characteristics of Middletonian verse, the prevalence of rhyme, varying length of line, an extraordinary fondness for triple endings, a slurring of syllables so as to crowd 14 or 15 or even more into the limits of a pentameter . . . , the use of words with a contracted "it" (such as "in't") to make double endings, the use of the Fletcherian extra emphatic syllable, and an occasional resort to a trochaic line after a double ending.

More importantly, says Oliphant, reverting to the subjective, "the resultant music is the same. . . . I attach more importance to the impression the verse makes upon me than I do to any other single factor." Back in the realm of the demonstrable, he cites a considerable number of "parallel passages"—short phrases which appear in similar form in the play in question and in Middleton's works. One illustration will perhaps suffice in place of Oliphant's seven pages of such parallels. Oliphant notes that both the author of *The Revenger's Tragedy* and Middleton are in the habit of "characterizing minutes and hours and days": for example, "this affecting minute" in Middleton's *The Fair Quarrel* and "false minute" in *The Revenger's Tragedy*. The article concludes with the unequivocal assertion that "Middleton was the author in *The Revenger's Tragedy*."[7]

Although good external evidence is generally given much greater weight than good internal evidence, there is no really good external proof in this case, as we have seen. Thus, Oliphant's citations of Middletonian parallels of verse and phrase are noteworthy.

Allardyce Nicoll, for one, took note. In what is still the definitive edition of the works of Tourneur, published three years after Oliphant's article, Nicoll reacts to the pressure to defend Tourneur's authorship in the light of Oliphant's work. First, he affirms the value of the Kirkman and Archer playlists. Then, after carefully giving Oliphant credit for his "painstaking care and acute observation," he discounts what he calls a "formidable list of 'echoes' and repetitions." Such echoes and repetitions, Nicoll asserts, are not a certain proof of common authorship. In other words, Oliphant has collected good internal evidence, but internal evidence itself is not a valid means of attribution. Unfortunately, what Nicoll himself seems to fall back on is perhaps even less valid: *The Atheist's Tragedy* and *The Revenger's Tragedy* share "something of the same spirit, something of the same mental processes, something of the same dark and ironical attitude towards life."[8] This is a legitimate *feeling*, but it does not amount to a *demonstration* of authorship.

How can the "spirit" of a play be measured and quantitatively compared? Can we really say that a work of art is revealing of the "mental processes" of its author? How many other Jacobean tragedies share "dark and ironical attitudes towards life?" Nicoll's argument here seems to imply what many years later he was to state overtly: that the play is Tourneur's until proved otherwise—as Tourneur's editor he has only to prove that a reasonable doubt exists to verify his attribution.[9]

Nicoll's edition of the *Works* was reviewed, quite favorably, by T. S. Eliot, in the (London) *Times Literary Supplement*. Eliot, like Nicoll, had been impressed but not convinced by Oliphant's evidence: "And in spite of Mr. Oliphant's weight of probabilities, there is one quality of Middleton which we do not find in the two plays attributed to Tourneur. The finest of the tragic characters of Middleton live in a way which differs from Tourneur's not in degree but in kind; and they have flashes of a kind of satiric wit unknown to Tourneur, in whom wit is supplied by a fierce grotesquerie." In addition to this negative evidence, Eliot briefly cites two more positive arguments: he trusts Nicoll and Sykes (who, it will be remembered, based his case on a faulty text), and, "what matters most is the beauty of the verse and the unity of the dramatic pattern of the two plays."[10] Eliot and Nicoll see clearly that the best refutation of the Middleton theory is to posit a relationship between *The Revenger's Tragedy* and *The Atheist's Tragedy*. Neither, however, is willing to go beyond a vague sentence or two in attempting to make this connection.

Eliot's review resulted in a brief flurry of controversy on the pages of subsequent issues of the (London) *Times Literary Supplement*. In a letter of December 11, 1930, Oliphant replies that he still champions Middleton, although he notes that "The author of *The Revenger's Tragedy* is markedly a moralist, as Middleton never is." Still, "I shall not really be convinced until the extraordinary similarities of tone, of expression, of syntax, and of vocabulary between this play and work of Middleton have been accounted for, as yet has not been done."[11] Eliot responds to Oliphant on January 1, 1931, noting that ". . . the differences between *The Revenger's Tragedy* and the whole of Middleton's work in tragedy are more significant than the differences between the two plays assigned to Tourneur."[12] Oliphant replied one month later. Then, for variety, some new voices are heard. On April 23, B. M. Wagner notes a

characteristic of Tourneur's spelling (adding an *h* to words that begin with an *a* such as "hability") which does not appear in *The Revenger's Tragedy*, nor in Middleton's works.[13] Finally, F. L. Jones, in the issue for June 18, offers another bit of evidence against Tourneur, based on the "use of the insignificant words *of* and *to* at the end of his lines."[14] It turns out that *The Atheist's Tragedy* ends lines with "of" twenty-seven times and with "to" nine times, whereas for *The Revenger's Tragedy* the figures are: "of" seven, "to" one. These figures, for what they are worth, are closer to Middleton's average usage of the words in comparable settings.

In 1935, nearly a decade after the article that touched off this flurry, Oliphant moves off the pages of the *TLS* to deliver the last word on "Tourneur and Mr. T. S. Eliot." He repeats his one doubt, based upon Tourneur's strong moralistic stance in *The Atheist's Tragedy* and Middleton's tendency to show "no concern whatever with moral problems." But, to convince him to change his mind, "some development from the one play to the other must be shown, but such development never has been shown, and, I venture to say, never can be shown."[15] Curiously, the years to come would see scholars attempting to demonstrate that Middleton was indeed a moralistic playwright, *and* that there was a strong connection between *The Atheist's Tragedy* and *The Revenger's Tragedy*. Both arguments therefore, would be turned around and used to prove the opposite of what Oliphant thinks they prove.

Meanwhile, during the years that the *TLS* controversy raged, an additional bit of Middletonian evidence was turned up. In 1927, H. N. Hillebrand published his discovery of a law suit in which Middleton figured prominently.[16] Middleton had been sued for debt by one M. Keysar, a theatrical entrepreneur. In defending himself, Middleton asserted that to satisfy the debt, he gave to Keysar, in 1606, the manuscript of a tragedy, *The Viper and Her Brood*. Hillebrand himself makes no connection between this play and Tourneur and *The Revenger's Tragedy*, but does note that the legal record suggests Middleton had been involved in the composition of at least one tragedy earlier than had previously been thought the case. This is immediately relevant to the controversy in that many of Tourneur's advocates had offered as evidence the "fact" that during the years *The Revenger's Tragedy* was written, produced, and printed, Middleton had been concerned solely with comedy. But *The Viper* soon came to play an even more important role. In 1931,

W. P. Dunkel sets out to reinforce Oliphant's case for Middleton. In addition to adding several parallel passages to Oliphant's already extensive list, Dunkel takes note of the recently discovered existence of *The Viper:* "No play entitled *The Viper and Her Brood* has come down to us, but one is tempted to ask whether this may not be merely another name for *The Revenger's Tragedy.*"[17] As Dunkel notes, there is a female character in the play of distinctly viperish quality, and with her sons and stepsons, she would well be called a "viper and her brood." Future advocates of the authorship of Middleton had another piece of ammunition—soldiers in the ranks of Tourneur now had another attack to repel.

V *Imagery*

The search for new angles of attack continues, and the next new development in this continuing argument proved something of an embarrassment for both sides. In 1935, U. Ellis-Fermor published her research into the question of authorship, employing "as the means for such an examination . . . Professor Caroline Spurgeon's illuminating studies of the imagery of Shakespeare's plays." Professor Spurgeon's method consisted of the search for patterns of "iterative imagery"—often repeated types of visual referents, which may be seen as clues to the mind and thought of the image maker. Ellis-Fermor examines *The Atheist's Tragedy* and *The Revenger's Tragedy,* and discovers similar images from building, from business, and from nature (especially rivers, streams, and winds). Moreover, both plays include two kinds of imagery, "one in which the imagery has the rare and sudden quality of inevitable poetry," and another with "a precision, an almost scientific exactness."[18] As a consequence of these similar patterns of image usage, Ellis-Fermor concludes that the same man—Tourneur—wrote both plays.

The relevance of Professor Spurgeon's studies of Shakespeare's iterative imagery to the Tourneur/Middleton controversy did not occur only to Ellis-Fermor. At about the same time she was working on Tourneur's imagery, Marco K. Mincoff addressed himself to the issue, noting that the sources of a dramatist's imagery should give a fairly accurate clue to his personality. Mincoff is particularly keen on the biographical implications of the Spurgeon technique: ". . . the main aim of the investigation must always be the discovery of facts about the author's personality and his type of mind."

Mincoff, like Ellis-Fermor, carefully analyzes the imagery of both plays. In addition, he adds for comparison the iterative imagery of Middleton, particularly in *Women Beware Women* and *The Changeling*. As can be seen by the fact that this study is about as long as the play it is about, Mincoff's work is exhaustive. He notes in *The Revenger's Tragedy* an "almost complete absence of all classical allusions," a "love of conceits of the metaphysical type," and a tendency to treat nature in an intellectual rather than visual manner. He concludes that the author of the work was a townsman.

In *The Atheist's Tragedy*, on the other hand, Mincoff finds longer and more labored images, based upon observation of the natural world rather than intellectualization of it: the author of this play (Tourneur) shows himself altogether less an urbanite. Middleton's imagery, on the other hand, shares with *The Revenger's Tragedy* brevity, force, urban preoccupations, and the intellectual rather than the visual perspective. The result—"a matter that must be evident to anyone who gives himself the trouble to compare the plays himself in the manner indicated"—is that Middleton is the author.

As if Fate were not satisfied with these two critics coming upon the same method and applying it simultaneously with diametrically opposed results, Mincoff, unaware of Ellis-Fermor's work, begins his article with a denunciation of all nonscientific evidence in this field: "what the value of a method of research is that admits of such conflicting results, that can at the will of the manipulator be applied to prove authorship . . . I may well leave to the parallel mongers themselves to define."[19] Rarely in real life does such sarcasm so quickly turn about to bite the hand that created it!

Twenty years later, Inga-stina Ekeblad (Ewebank) again approached the imagery of the play to search there for a clue to its authorship. Ekeblad, however, attempts "a *functional* approach to Tourneur's images." She finds that "there are important similarities in the use to which imagery is put in the two plays, in the function of imagery as part of dramatic structure and technique." In both *The Revenger's Tragedy* and *The Atheist's Tragedy*, imagery is put to moral use and "each is organized by the idea of the *exemplum horrendum.*" On the other hand, there are also differences in the functional uses of imagery in the two plays: in *The Atheist's Tragedy* imagery is carefully "constructed to conduct a kind of argument," while "in *The Revenger's Tragedy* we are asked for immediate responses to the evils that are being demonstrated."

Curiously, Ekeblad considers this difference to be as much a demonstration of common authorship as the similarities: it shows that Tourneur carefully employed imagery in a way that related to the specific function of both plays: "A study of the imagery of *The Revenger's Tragedy* and *The Atheist's Tragedy*, then, shows a firm integration, a unity of aim, of the imagery with the dramatic structure and technique. It shows Tourneur to be alert to some important dramatic uses of imagery."[20] It is possible for the cynic to ask if the ability to use images in a manner which is organically related to the function of the play is a sufficiently unique characteristic of Tourneur to be of much use in determining authorship. But at any rate, no studies appeared simultaneously with Ekeblad's which attempted to prove, through a functional approach to imagery, that Tourneur did *not* write the play.

VI *Moral Developmentalists*

Oliphant, the strongest early advocate of Middleton, suggested repeatedly that it was not possible to argue for Tourneur, unless some development of thought could be traced from *The Revenger's Tragedy* to *The Atheist's Tragedy*. Beginning in the late 1930s (and continuing to the present time), a number of champions have entered the arena to take this challenge.

In 1938, L. G. Salingar[21] points the way for future students by noting the influence of the medieval morality play tradition in *The Revenger's Tragedy* (as well as *The Atheist's Tragedy*, and surprisingly, *The Transformed Metamorphosis*). Two years later, Harold Jenkins speaks more formally to the question of development: ". . . between the composition of the two plays his mind progressed enormously. In *The Atheist's Tragedy* an instinctive disgust with humanity has been replaced by a searching inquiry into the foundations of human life, a desire to understand its purpose and to formulate a view of man's position in the universe." Jenkins compares the "energetic, fiery, rapid, and passionate" style of *The Revenger's Tragedy* to the "slow reflectiveness" and "masterly lucidity" of *The Atheist's Tragedy*. The plot of the former is a kind of outburst of passion, while that of the latter is "not so much a plot wrought by the imagination as one intellectually constructed to develop a certain train of thought." Unlike Middleton's characters, says Jenkins, Tourneur's have an awareness of sin. The plays move from passion to reason, but both deal with the role of sin in human life: "Instinctively passion has given way to thought, and the effort to express thought has left its mark on every detail of *The Atheist's Tragedy*, from the manipulation of the plot and characters to the structure of the verse."[22]

Like Salingar, T. M. Parrott and R. H. Ball see *The Revenger's Tragedy* in relation to *The Transformed Metamorphosis:* the play "is the dramatization of the vision obscurely apprehended in Tourneur's first poem." The vision is of

a world corrupted by gold and lust, and lying under the shadow of death. But there is more in the poem than this general satire; appended to it is a bit of allegory quite in the manner of Spenser. Something of this curious juxtaposition—it cannot be called a blend—of Marston's obsession with vice, and Spenser's worship of chaste beauty, appears in much of Tourneur's work, more particularly in his first play.[23]

H. H. Adams also argues for Tourneur's authorship on the basis of a moral development; specifically, a development of the theme of revenge. The two plays "possess a common approach to the problem of revenge, and . . . together they present a single mind's ordered view of the universe." In *The Revenger's Tragedy*, "Active personal vengeance of any type is rejected, death being the invariable lot of any who take this route, and Tourneur makes it clear that such vengeance is directly opposed to God's law." While in *The Atheist's Tragedy*, "Tourneur sets himself the task of dramatizing the conclusion he had already reached in *The Revenger's Tragedy*. The two plays, therefore, can and should be taken together—as the work of one author—presenting 'a study of revenge in its entirety.' "[24]

This contention, and its brother—that Tourneur is responsible for the contested work since Middleton neglects moral problems in his plays—are questioned by Samuel Schoenbaum. The author of *The Revenger's Tragedy*, Schoenbaum contends, "is interested not in how the good man prospers but in how the wicked man sets in motion the forces that will, in the end, destroy him. This pattern is demonstrated constantly in the plays of Thomas Middleton and becomes the essence of his moral system." Moreover, this moral pattern, "so apparent in *The Revenger's Tragedy* and in Middleton's acknowledged plays, cannot be inferred from any of Tourneur's unquestioned works."[25]

Schoenbaum, at this point in time, however, seems to be a lone

voice in the critical wilderness. Advocates of Tourneur's authorship
have at last mustered some new evidence of their own, and discussions of the moral development from one play to the other roll on.
Indeed, two years after Schoenbaum's note, one critic could boldly
cite similarities of "moral attitudes" between the two plays with no
amplifying details.[26]
    Several important works of the 1950s and 1960s stress the moral
development from *The Revenger's Tragedy* to *The Atheist's
Tragedy*. Robert Ornstein suggests that

Tourneur's intellectual and spiritual roots were in a pre-Renaissance past.
The medieval cast of his thought is evident in most of his works—in his
predilection for allegory and in his preoccupation with the terms of *vanitas*,
memento mori, and *contemptus mundi*. A literalistic religious viewpoint is,
of course, far more apparent in *The Atheist's Tragedy* than in *The Revenger's Tragedy*, but even in the latter, the degeneracy of the world is
measured by its divergence from a medieval conception of the universe as
the theatre of God's judgment.

The Atheist's Tragedy, in Ornstein's view returns, to the orthodoxy
of Tourneur's fundamental position.[27] It is a "product of the same
mind and talent which created *The Revenger's Tragedy*."[28]
    Like Salingar and Ornstein, J. D. Peter attributes the play to
Tourneur on the basis of a moral progression which is basically
medieval. Both plays are "set against the fabric of Christian Ethics,"
The Revenger's Tragedy in particular being based on a tradition of
satiric and religious literature[29] and having obvious parallels with
The Atheist's Tragedy. The second work, in turn, has "obvious
points of contact with the tradition of Complaint . . . which tend to
confirm a reading of *The Revenger's Tragedy* as something more
than cynical." *The Atheist's Tragedy* is an aid to understanding *The
Revenger's Tragedy*.[30]
    In 1960, Inga-Stina Ekeblad (whom we have seen already as an
advocate of Tourneur from the perspective of image studies) again
considers the question of relationship to earlier literary traditions:
she finds a "fusion of various traditional dramatic forms, each with
its own characteristic mode of expression." There are three of these
traditions, the revenge play, the dramatic satire, and the morality
play (that is, the elements discussed, respectively, by Adams, Peter,
and Salingar). *The Atheist's Tragedy* also develops within these

three traditional modes, and adds a fourth: the study of the Christian-Stoic hero. Both plays, then, are "conceived and constructed on the basis of traditional Christian morality."[31] Contrary to Professor Schoenbaum, Ekeblad finds nary a trace of "inherent moral purpose" in Middleton's early works: *The Revenger's Tragedy*, therefore, is by Tourneur.

Irving Ribner is, to date, the last major critic to make a case for Tourneur's authorship of *The Revenger's Tragedy* upon that play's moral similarity to *The Atheist's Tragedy:* "What is perhaps even more striking about these two plays is that each in its own way is a highly moralistic and didactic work, and that they share a crusading missionary tone and a common point of view which renders them more like one another than either is like any of the plays of Tourneur's contemporaries." This common point of view, Professor Ribner finds, is based upon a belief in the virtues of primitive Christianity.[32] This belief is manifested through the development of the revenge motif: "private revenge was condemned as morally wrong, a sin directly against God. . . . An awareness of this ethical conviction is crucial to an understanding of both of Tourneur's plays. It is basic to *The Revenger's Tragedy*. . . ."[33]

I suspect that when Oliphant, in the 1920s and 1930s demanded, rhetorically, that the advocates of Tourneur in this authorship controversy show some proof of relationship between the two plays, he hardly suspected twenty years of response. While there remained many who were totally unconvinced by this flood of evidence, none would deny its value. Unlike metrical tests, attempts to show the development of some strain of moral thought from *The Revenger's Tragedy* to *The Atheist's Tragedy* have, almost coincidentally, refocused critical attention on the plays themselves. From such studies much of value can be learned about the two tragedies as works of art, regardless of the authorship issue.

VII *Mid-century Miscellany*

Although the champions of Tourneur's authorship have concentrated on the question of moral development from one play to the other they have not neglected other promising fields of inquiry. Perhaps most notable among the new areas is one which might be called "theatrical evidence." During the years of the contested work's production and printing, Middleton seems to have been working solely for the Children's Companies of players, and hence it is to the advantage of the advocates of Tourneur to show that *The Revenger's Tragedy* was not written for these companies.

Inga-Stina Ekeblad takes just this approach, attempting to "point to an external fact which suggests that *The Revenger's Tragedy* not only belonged to the King's Men at the time of its printing, but was actually written for performance at the Globe viz. the appearance in the play of a blazing star."[34] This particular stage effect, she notes, was a well-known specialty of the Globe theater and the King's Men, and not used by the Children's Companies. Therefore, the play is by Tourneur, since it is not by Middleton.

Other critics on the Tourneur side continue to mention this evidence, until it assumes the character of unchanging and eternal truth. Thus, as late as 1966, R. A. Foakes cites in behalf of Tourneur that "*The Revenger's Tragedy* was acted by the King's Men, at a time when Middleton is not known to have any connection with them, and when he was, indeed, a principal author for their rivals, the Children's Companies."[35] Of course, this fact was available, on the title page of the 1607–1608 quarto edition of the play where, for example, Archer and Kirkman could well have noted it when compiling their seventeenth-century playlists. At best, then, the new theatrical evidence on the authorship of *The Revenger's Tragedy* merely corroborates what seems to have been generally assumed for three and a half centuries, namely, that the play was in fact, as it claimed to be, produced at the Globe theater by the King's Men.

At this point, it should come as no surprise to anyone that arguments for Middleton's authorship of the play were also being put forward in the middle years of this century. Curiously, the two sides seem to have shifted critical positions. After the burst of new "evidence" for Middleton in the 1920s and 1930s, critics of the next three decades who advocate Middleton's authorship seem content to rehash older types of evidence, while during these same years, the Tourneur camp was developing and pushing the new moral development argument.

In 1945 R. H. Barker lists seven sorts of evidence for Middleton, most of which are already painfully familiar: he cites parallels of ironic patterns; stylistic parallels; diction parallels; parallel mannerisms such as "characterizing minutes, hours and days"; versification tests; the uses of oaths and ejaculations: and parallel phrases.[36]

A decade later, Barker is still as convinced of Middleton's responsibility for *The Revenger's Tragedy,* but bases his case almost wholly on "new evidence that will, I think, settle the controversy about authorship once and for all." This evidence turns out to be the relationship between the hero of the play and Middleton's comic heroes. Vindice closely resembles ". . . Follywit in *A Mad World, My Masters.* For Vindice is now shown to be another example of the clever man who is blinded by his own cleverness, the self-satisfied hero who turns out to be anything but a hero in the end. The plays in which he and Follywit appear are in fact companion pieces and quite obviously—if the reader takes the trouble to compare them— the work of the same man."[37] Unfortunately, Barker's hopes of ending the controversy once and for all were not to be satisfied. His "new evidence" is strikingly similar to that offered seven years earlier by S. Schoenbaum in "*The Revenger's Tragedy* and Middleton's Moral Outlook" (see above p. 71).

Schoenbaum himself reappears in the mid-fifties, still as a champion of Middleton in *Middleton's Tragedies* (dedicated to R. H. Barker). On this occasion Schoenbaum reveals in his detailed and careful argument a sense of restraint and an unwillingness to view his evidence as finally conclusive—qualities which are sadly lacking in most participants in the Tourneur-Middleton controversy: "The case for Middleton's authorship is, I believe, sufficiently strong to warrant including *The Revenger's Tragedy*—at least tentatively— among the acknowledged plays in the canon of his works." After a careful—and refreshingly balanced—review of the argument to date, he bases his attribution on the association of *The Revenger's Tragedy* and *The Viper and Her Brood;* the play's moral point of view; uses of irony; parallels of verbal mannerisms; metrical evidence; and parallels of expression.[38]

The internal evidence supplied by such parallels of phraseology continues to be gathered. One rather small piece is introduced in 1960 by M. P. Jackson:

The theory that Middleton rather than Tourneur wrote *The Revenger's Tragedy* is thus supported by the fact that "Ay" is greatly predominant over "Yes" in this play, which is generally dated 1606–1607, whereas "Yes" is the almost invariable affirmative particle in the only play of which Tourneur's authorship is undoubted. The relevant figures follow

   The Atheist's Tragedy: "Ay" 4, "Yes" 21
   The Revenger's Tragedy: "Ay" 27, "Yes" 5
   Middleton's *Phoenix:* "Ay" 27, "Yes" 6[39]

Studies of this sort of linguistic parallels between *The Revenger's Tragedy* and Middleton's works reach some sort of apotheosis in Peter Murray's *A Study of Cyril Tourneur*. The section of Murray's book in which he deals with this authorship issue looks—and at times, reads—like a textbook in mathematical statistical analysis. But, although the numbers are different, the tune is the same: Murray compiles data on "the frequency of occurence of certain pronouns, verb forms and colloquial contractions . . . by introducing separate analyses for preferred spellings and for preferred linguistic forms. Thus modified, the method yields results leaving little doubt that Thomas Middleton and not Cyril Tourneur is the author."[40] Curiously, the sense of certainty manifested in the last sentence of the above passage seems to desert Murray at an odd moment. After mustering what is truly an impressive compilation of data "proving" Middleton the author of *The Revenger's Tragedy*, Murray judiciously determines that there is just enough doubt left to enable him to discuss the meaning of the play for the next eighty pages of his 275-page book on Tourneur.

A slightly different sort of evidence for Middleton's authorship was introduced in 1960 by George R. Price, who approaches the fray from the perspective of a descriptive bibliographer—a student of printing practices. He concludes that *The Revenger's Tragedy* was printed, more or less accurately, from a manuscript in the author's own hand. He suspects that this is also the case of the unquestioned Tourneur works. Since there exists undeniable evidence of Middleton's holographic habits, Price proceeds to compare *The Revenger's Tragedy* to the work of the contending authors. He concentrates on act and scene divisions, "the use of mere numbers as speech headings," habitual patterns of punctuation, and spelling.[41] Price's methodology seems, at present, more suggestive than conclusive. As proof positive, a chain of deductions can only go on for a limited time before one begins to suspect that somewhere along the line there almost has to be a weak link. Nevertheless, this approach seems to offer some possible directions for future scholars who wish to break new ground in the authorship controversy—assuming that any scholars exist now or will exist in the future who are not thoroughly weary of this whole business.

VIII *Anon, Anon*

In fact, although history has invariably proved wrong those who declared this controversy at an end, it does seem that at least the intensity of the fray has been diminishing. An entirely new trend seems to be developing concerning the authorship of *The Revenger's Tragedy*. This trend is the wholesome and highly welcomed profession of ultimate ignorance concerning the identity of the author of the play. In one sense, modern students of the problem are rediscovering Oliphant's attribution of the play to that most prolific of Renaissance authors, "Anon."

Schoenbaum, earlier one of the most persuasive advocates of Middleton's authorship, writes "neither Middleton's nor Tourneur's advocates have been able to bring forward the kind of proof to which one party or the other must submit. . . . Hence the seemingly endless exchange of replies and counterreplies in the journals. Whatever his own personal *feeling* about the attribution may be, the task of the historian is, as I see it, to record the fact of uncertainty, which is in this case the only certainty."[42]

Noting that "the progress of the Tourneur-Middleton controversy has been marked time and again by the simultaneous appearance of confident statements wholly opposed to each other and hence mutually contradictory,"[43] Allardyce Nicoll, a combatant from the Tourneur side, joins Schoenbaum in sensible retreat. Nicoll's position is stated in an article which is appropriately entitled "*The Revenger's Tragedy* and the Virtue of Anonymity."

Perhaps it is appropriate that a recent editor of the play, Lawrence J. Ross, should have the last word: "Studies based on literary evidence, then, have not produced an overwhelmingly convincing case for either Tourneur or Middleton. . . . In sum, the present editor can state with some confidence that he does not know who wrote *The Revenger's Tragedy*."[44]

To return for a moment to Professor Schoenbaum's distinction, the present writer *feels* that Tourneur wrote *The Revenger's Tragedy*. But this feeling cannot be proved. Indeed, it seems that the careful historian of this controversy can only conclude that, after a century of contradictory certainties, no one came close to proving who wrote the play, and unless dramatic new evidence (probably of an external type) is discovered, no one ever will. What, then, are we to do with *The Revenger's Tragedy*? It seems that there are two options. It is, of course, possible to simply pretend that it is a totally anonymous work—although almost everyone who has studied the play concludes that it is either by Tourneur or Middleton. As such, it could only be discussed in isolation, never to be related—at least through shared authorship—to the other works of any one author.

This is a tempting approach. It satisfies the new critical doctrine of independent Aristotelian analysis of every work of art, and it closes the book on the whole question of authorship. But such an approach seems also unproductive and unrealistic.

In fact, *The Revenger's Tragedy* is probably by either Middleton or Tourneur. Perhaps the best that can be done is to accept this one undisputed fact in the spirit of compromise. Those who wish to discuss the play in the context of Middleton's works should do so, noting that this attribution is only a potential one. Those who wish to treat the play as Tourneur's should also do so, with the same note. Working from such a position, presumably no one would be so rash as to make a major portion of his interpretation of either dramatist stand or fall on the basis of his candidate's authorship of *The Revenger's Tragedy*. In Schoenbaum's revised edition of the *Annals of English Drama*, the author of *The Revenger's Tragedy* is listed as "Anonymous (Tourneur, C.? Middleton, T.?)."[45] Perhaps that is where the matter should end.

CHAPTER 4

The Revenger's Tragedy: *Meaning*

I "*Blood, Lust, and Morbid Passions*"

THE *Revenger's Tragedy* is a play in which evil people and evil actions are a central concern. Critics and students of English Renaissance drama have long been fascinated by this tragedy, and much of their interest has focused on the work's moral dimension. Nineteenth- and early twentieth-century critics were particularly struck with the dark world of the play, and concentrated their attentions almost exclusively upon its "atmosphere of blood, lust, and morbid passions."[1] They found an "insidious pessimism"[2] in its "stale and acrid flavor of decadent Italianism."

More recent critics also have occasionally seen the play as uncompromisingly morally bleak. U. Ellis-Fermor, for example, says that "Tourneur, thus excluding from his mind and ours pity and that part of normal tragic fear which is sympathy leaves us face to face with a form of horror that is in tragedy the logical inference from a universe denuded of spiritual significance."[3]

Perhaps the apotheosis of this view of the play as a work obsessed with dark themes and animated by an unremitting pessimism is that of T. S. Eliot:

The cynicism, the loathing and disgust of humanity, expressed consummately in *The Revenger's Tragedy*, are immature in the respect that they exceed the object. Their objective equivalents are characters practising the grossest vices; characters that seem merely to be spectres projected from the poet's inner world, some horror beyond words. So the play is a document on one human being, Tourneur; its motive is truly the death motive, for it is the loathing and horror of life itself. To have realized this motive so well is a triumph; for the hatred of life is an important phase—even, if you like, a mystical experience—in life itself.[4]

Eliot's essay, for all its brilliance, points to two chief objections to

79

this species of Tourneur criticism. In the first place, the essay pre-supposes that the attitudes and feelings of the play's characters (par-ticularly Vindice, the play's chief character) are the attitudes and feelings of the playwright himself ("projected from the poet's inner world of nightmare"). Second, in stressing the vigor and personal nature of the play, Eliot and many other critics neglect the play's real and multiple indebtedness to traditional literary and social con-ventions and structures, and hence the moral framework which sur-rounds the work's "world of nightmare."

The first of these fallacies is as easy to expose as it is difficult to dispel. Drama, by its very nature, is without an authorial "point of view." Any given play is a complex of points of view, each character, in effect, speaking for himself. Clearly, in some plays, the evidence of the work itself makes it apparent that some characters represent positions closer to that of the author than do others: Iago's point of view cannot easily be mistaken for Shakespeare's. In fact, however, the same may be said of Othello. There is no major character in this particular drama who speaks for the author. Rather, the point of view of Othello emerges from the interplay of both words and ac-tions of all the play's characters. Similarly, those who see in The Revenger's Tragedy a wholly morbid and pessimistic immersion into a world of unrelieved sin exclude the possibility that the play is a balanced and coherent work of art, written by an artist with an acute sense of the conventions of the Elizabethan tragic drama, and the tradition from which it arose.

Modern criticism of The Revenger's Tragedy has turned to this "tradition" and discovered that it is not a tradition, but several traditions, traditions that are moralistic and conservative. An under-standing of these conventional elements suggests that the play is anything but a neurotic self-portrait written by a narrow and ob-sessed fatalist.

II *Italy and the Italianate*

Perhaps the most obvious convention operating in the play is that of place: "The scene of *The Revenger's Tragedy* is that Italy which Elizabethans regarded with mingled horror and fascination. 'O Italie,' exclaims Nashe, 'the Academie of man-slaughter. . . .' "[5] The Italy of Renaissance England, somewhat like the South of early twentieth-century American literature, is a fantasy world with some relationship to reality. In many ways, this "Italy" is a dark reflection of the brutal and grotesque Italy of the later Middle Ages and Renaissance. Plots filled with Italian horrors such as that of Webster's *The White Devil* and perhaps even *The Revenger's Tragedy* itself, all too frequently turn out to be not the products of a deformed imagination, but a retelling of actual historical events. Professors S. Schoenbaum and N. W. Bawcutt, for example, find striking parallels between Tourneur's gruesome plot and the historical records of the Medicis, while L. G. Salingar finds similar parallels to the family of Estensi.[6]

The occasional resemblances between an historical Italy and an English literary Italy do not, however, change the fact that the setting of this drama and other Italianate plays of the period is primarily a convention. Italians, according to this convention, "are vainglorious, vengeful, treacherous, factious, dissembling, lustful and adulterous."[7] Italy—seen by newly Protestant England as the seat of ungodly Catholicism—was the seedbed and showplace of every imaginable depravity and vice. The art of murder, ingenious poisonings in particular, was considered the specialty of the Italians—witness the original and bizarre murders of *The White Devil.*[8]

In short, the corruption of the Italianate court of the play is hardly to be ascribed to the depraved imagination of Tourneur. Rather, Tourneur is "distilling the essence of Italianate horror, by preempting and refining a conventional image of sensuality and violence."[9] The world of *The Revenger's Tragedy* is indeed a dark universe— one in which the basest passions and cruelest tastes of mankind grow and flourish like a crop of grisly mushrooms in a dark and damp cellar. But from the moment a Renaissance audience grasped the setting of the play, they expected such a universe. This audience might expect differences in the types of evil exemplified by the drama's characters, but they would not expect moral gradations from good to evil. Rather, virtually every character in the play, including its protagonists, would be evil, and totally so.

III *Morality and Morality Plays*

The expectation of the kind of moral absolutes encouraged by the Italianate setting is reinforced by other literary conventions found in *The Revenger's Tragedy.* Many critics have discerned in the play reminders of the medieval English morality plays, in which allegorical personifications of vices and virtues battled for the soul of an

Everyman. The self-defining names of Tourneur's characters (Lussurioso: "lecherous"; Spurio: "bastard"; Ambitioso: "ambitious"; Vindice: "a revenger"; Gratiana: "grace"; Castiza: "chaste"; Piato: "hidden") "go back to the medieval tradition of allegory, and especially to the morality plays, with their Wanton, Lust, and Iniquity."[10] Inga-Stina Ekeblad finds *The Revenger's Tragedy* "organized by the idea of the *exemplum horrendum* . . ."[11]—a model of a life which leads to damnation—which she traces back to the morality plays.

The implications of the influence of the morality plays upon Tourneur's work are many and important. At the simplest level, the influence again reinforces the view of Tourneur as conscious artist selectively exploring and utilizing elements of his literary heritage—in other words, an artist like T. S. Eliot—not the possessed and obsessive wild man pictured by Eliot and the earlier critics. *The Revenger's Tragedy* should be considered as a work of literature, not as the literary autobiography of an author caught in the web of an adolescent view of the world as evil.

Moreover, this influence suggests that Tourneur was not only a conscious literary artist, but, in terms of his artistic antecedents, a conservative artist at that (again like Eliot or the early Shakespeare). By 1600 the morality play was an archaic dramatic form. Tourneur has gone back to the primary form of the drama of one hundred years before the Jacobean era for important elements of his plot, his characters, and his theme.

This literary conservatism reflects a moral or theological conservatism: "Tourneur is unique in his age for the moral fervor with which he uses the drama to espouse a primitive Christianity more closely related to that of the medieval world than to that of the seventeenth century."[12] Not only does Tourneur utilize the form of the morality plays, he also makes use of the *morality* of the morality play: "The degeneracy of the world is measured by its divergence from a medieval conception of the universe as the Theater of God's judgment."[13]

The medieval morality of this play is revealed in the ambiguity of the title: Is this a tragedy wrought by a revenger or is it the tragedy of the revenger himself? Clearly, it is both. Vindice is an instrument of revenge, and he successfully purges the duke's court of many if not all of its evil characters. Given the Italianate environment within which the action of the work is set, a scourge like Vindice probably represents the only viable human agent of moral order. But Vindice, or personified human revenge, as an instrument for the restoration of moral order is inevitably flawed. In the process of gaining his revenge, Vindice must enter the evil world of those upon whom he would be revenged. If murder is a sin, and must be revenged, the vengeful murderer is by definition a sinner. Murray observes: "To transform evil into good, Vindice enters upon a course of action in which he transforms good into evil; as he purges the court, he creates a terrible darkness in his own soul."[14] Finally, of course, Vindice is himself destroyed, at least in part as a result of a system of retributive justice he has himself initiated.

What makes this denunciation of human justice and revenge medieval, of course, is that it is based soundly on the important canon of medieval Christianity that God's is the only real justice; that "Vengeance is mine, saith the Lord"; that, as another Renaissance revenger learned and Vindice never did, it is not the role of man to seek justice through revenge but to wait and learn to recognize that "special providence in the fall of the sparrow."

IV *The Irony of Revenge*

It is this conflict between human revenge and divine punishment which generates the system of ironies critics have noted in *The Revenger's Tragedy*. Each and every act of human vengeance attempted in the play does not work as the revenger(s) plan. Rather, such actions always tend to further the cause of legitimate justice— quite against their actor's wills. As P. Lisca has observed, "It is difficult to see where Tourneur has missed a single opportunity for ironic reversal and it is the ubiquitousness of the irony which imparts, even to the plot, a sense of unity."[15]

The ends of human justice in *The Revenger's Tragedy* are inevitably more "just" than they were conceived to be. The irony arises as divine justice thwarts human revenge, as the evil plans of evil characters become twisted toward good. Clearly some sort of cosmic moral order is at work when, for example, Supervacuo and Ambitioso play the role of sympathetic brothers while they try to have Lussurioso executed, and produce instead the much deserved execution of their own real brother. This configuration is related in its irony to the situation in Chaucer's "Pardoner's Tale" in which the evil Pardoner, with the most selfish and sinful goals, tells a moral tale which may be a powerful force to move his auditors toward virtue.

We are reminded of the overtly metaphysical and Christian nature of this moral order with each appearance of Vindice's mother, Gratiana. The name "Gratiana" is derived from the word "grace" and it is some measure of the gulf between human and divine justice in this work that Vindice can say "Save Grace the bawde I seldom heare Grace nam'd!" (I. iii. 18). Nevertheless, it is Gratiana alone of all the minor characters in the drama who demonstrates the workings of divine justice. She alone transforms evil into good, without attempting to resort to human vengeance. After she has been corrupted by Vindice, Gratiana seems to personify the lowest depths to which a human being can fall in the deformed world of *The Revenger's Tragedy*. She *is* "Grace the bawde." But when confronted with evidence of her fall, she behaves as a true Christian—she confesses her sin, repents of it, and does penance. This seems to be the alternative Tourneur offers to Vindice's notion of the pursuit of justice and the elimination of sin and sinners. Gratiana, by confessing and repenting for her sin, is appealing to God's grace. Vindice takes upon himself the implementation of justice, rather than trusting to God, and he damns himself in the process. It is no accident that in the final murderous masque the disguised Vindice is indistinguishable—in costume *and* motivation—from his worst enemies.

It is clear that this interplay between human justice and divine justice is dependent upon the concept of revenge. Tourneur makes of revenge the ultimate in human justice—the wronged man acting as judge, prosecutor, and executioner. Tourneur's treatment of the morality of revenge, and the roles of man and God in executing it, is clearly within another literary convention, that of the revenge tragedy.

Although several critics have touched upon *The Revenger's Tragedy* as revenge play,[16] perhaps the most important aspect of the drama as revenge play lies in this focus on the limitations of human justice in a world presided over by a just God. The Jacobean stage had seen the conventions of the tragedy of revenge utilized often as a convenient mode for the presentation of bloody and exciting melodramatic spectacles, but the serious moral issues raised by human revenge had been an intimate part of the convention since its origins as well. The two most important revenge plays of the English Renaissance drama confirm the conventionality of this theme.

Kyd's *The Spanish Tragedy*, the first and perhaps most influential English play of this genre, is about justice. Hieronimo, the play's revenger hero, is ironically a minister of justice who, when wronged, attempts to administer justice himself through revenge. But Hieronimo is plagued by doubts of the legitimacy of his plan:

> Vindicti mihi!
> Ay, heaven will be revenged of every ill,
> Nor will they suffer murder unrepaid.
> Then stay, Hieronimo, attend their will:
> For mortal man may not appoint their time.
>
> (III. xiv. 1–5)

Hieronimo, in effect, takes a moral position somewhere between Vindice and Tourneur. Like Vindice, he sees revenge as one way a wronged human being can achieve justice, and like Vindice, Hieronimo does not long survive those upon whom he has taken his vengeance. But like Tourneur, and unlike Vindice, Hieronimo has grave doubts about the morality of his actions within a divine system of law and justice.

Hamlet, of course, is also a revenger who doubts the ethics of revenge. Surely this doubt is one of the reasons behind his much discussed procrastination. It is only when he submits to his fortune and allows himself to be exiled that he comes to realize, through the lucky "accidents" on his way to England, that

> Our indiscretion sometime serves us well
> When our deep plots do pall, and that should learn us
> There's a divinity that shapes our ends,
> Rough-hew them how we will.
>
> (V. ii. 8–11)

Both Hieronimo and Hamlet do eventually administer the longed for revenge, but both are impotent until they realize that they can only act as divine scourges, tools in the hand of a just God. But, even as divine instruments, both are sullied by their vengeance and die with their victims. Vindice never asked the questions of Hamlet or Hieronimo, but Tourneur did. He arrived at an answer more orthodox, more medieval, more Christian, and more positive than did Shakespeare and Kyd. In doing so, of course, he reduces the scope of human potential to just the extent that he advances the power of the divine. Vindice is no Hamlet, hardly a Hieronimo, precisely because he is never plagued with the questions his creator has already answered. At its origins and at its highest development, the English revenge play exists in a state of tension: it questions the ethics upon which its plot depends. *The Revenger's Tragedy* is both the logical continuation of this literary tradition and its last step: it does not question those ethics, but denies them totally.

V *Satire*

In his role as revenger, then, Vindice, like the hero of a morality play, chooses between allegorized vices (Ambitioso, Supervacuo, et al.) and Virtues (Gratiana), and makes the wrong choice. In a world which can be ruled only by God's judgment, he places his trust, through the vengeance ethic, in human justice—a justice which is here consistently and ironically twisted to serve a higher end. In his role as miguided executor of justice, Vindice sees his environment (rightly) as morally polluted and himself (wrongly) as the scourge of that pollution. But Tourneur's hero does not simply see evil, and act to try to eliminate it: he also comments upon his observations. Vindice occupies a unique position within *The Revenger's Tragedy* in his relationship to the audience, a position as conventional as the hero of a morality play, but as contemporary as his other position is archaic: Vindice is a satirist.

We have observed in Chapter 2 some of the features of conventional Jacobean satire in connection with Tourneur's earlier nondramatic works. This satire takes as its aim the exposure of human vice as manifested in a degenerated society. Satirists of the era of King James I worked within both dramatic and nondramatic modes, as did Tourneur, but, naturally, dramatic satire makes certain special demands. Of these, perhaps the most important is the demand of a satiric voice, or, more simply, a satirist.

In nondramatic satire, of course, the poet can himself play the role of satirist: he can re-create imaginatively the fallen world, and analyze it as well. For it is implicit in satire that the fallen world has in fact fallen from something. The evils that the satirist presents us must be understood in terms of the virtues they violate. The nondramatic satirist, by pointing out this divergence, by making moral comments on it, can assure himself that his audience "gets the point." The dramatist, however, since he lacks a "point of view," is faced with the problem of convincing his audience that the fallen world he presents in fact diverges from an ideal, and is not simply the imaginative construction of a totally evil universe.

One way to solve this problem, the way Tourneur and many other Jacobean dramatists chose, was to write into a play a character who performs the role of the satirist. Such a character participates in the play's action, and comments upon it—he is something of a chorus, standing between the audience and the action.

It is really not surprising that the hero of a tragedy of revenge should play the additional role of satirist. As a revenger, such a hero is usually in the position of a "moral purger of a corrupt court," a role that Vindice certainly tries to play (as do Hieronimo and Hamlet).[17]

Congruent with this role, the revenger-satirist will have constant opportunity to comment upon the corruption he is to purge. If Vindice fails in his role as purger, he certainly succeeds in his position of commentator and thoroughly convinces us that his environment is indeed a degenerate one.

The satirical Vindice is at the forefront from the very first line of the play. The first fifty-three lines of *The Revenger's Tragedy*— while they serve other functions as well—are sharply satiric. Vindice describes and curses most of the principals of the Duke's court, and comments specifically upon the nature of their transgressions:

> O that marrow-lesse age,
> Would stuffe the hollow Bones with dambd desires,
> And stead of heate kindle infernall fires,
> Within the spend-thift veynes of a drye Duke,
> A parcht and juicelesse luxor. O God! one
> That has scarce bloud inough to live upon.
> And hee to ryot it like a sonne and heyre?
>
> (I. i. 5–11)

This is, of course, exposition—it tells us what kind of character the Duke may be expected to be. But it is also much more general satiric comment. Vindice is attacking intemperate old age, specifically, sexual lust—"dambd desires . . . infernall fires"—in one who is "parcht and juicelesse." We have already seen this vice attacked in *The Transformed Metamorphosis*, and it is worth noting that it is a symbolic sort of vice. Tourneur seems to feel that when old men fall prey to lust—generally a young man's crime—then the world is indeed transformed into a grotesque reverse image of the ideal. Vindice suggests the more proper behavior of a man the Duke's age in the phrase "stead of heate," which is set in apposition to "infernal fires"—the gentle warmth of an ideal old age opposed to the transformed lust of a geriatric "luxor." Through his choice of imagery, moreover, Vindice suggests that this particular sin violates the natural limits of the human body: "stuffe the hollow Bones . . . spend-thrift veynes . . . parcht and juiceless . . . scarce bloud inough to live upon."

In line 11, Vindice shifts his metaphysical ground, and describes the aged lecher as a riotous heir. This is the first step along a well-traveled path in *The Revenger's Tragedy*, the coupling of the sexual and fiscal irresponsibility, of spiritual and material decay. Just a few lines later in this satiric monologue, we meet the "Usurers sonne" who will "melt all his patrimony in a kisse . . ." (29–30), and later we are warned that "Age as in gold, in lust is covetous" (42).

It is appropriate that this rather abstracted bit of satirical description occurs in the very first lines of the play. It sets the tone for much satirical comment later, and it neatly begins to define the complex character of the play's protagonist.

In this context, it is worth noting that Tourneur makes use of "theatrical imagery" as well as "verbal imagery" to make his point.[18] From Vindice's words we can see that he will stand between the play and its audience in the position of moral commentator upon both action and character. The staging of this scene makes the same point in nonverbal imagery. Tourneur has constructed the scene in such a way as to make necessary an arrangement of actors on stage whereby Vindice can see the procession of Duke, Duchess, et al. (as can the audience). But he must also be in a position to comment freely upon the procession without interfering with it or being heard by those about whom he comments. Thus, it is almost a necessity that Vindice literally be standing between the audience and the courtly procession. He is in front stage center, looking at both the courtly procession to the rear of the stage and the audience directly in front of him. In his opening monologue, Vindice is physically as well as verbally assuming the position of the satirist, positioned between that which is satirized and those for whom the satire is written.

Although Vindice's opening soliloquy is a notable illustration of the satiric principle operating in *The Revenger's Tragedy*, it is only an opening. From beginning to end, this is a play concerned with the revelation and description of a corrupt society. The specific villainies scourged by the satirist are predictable and conventional:

we have already observed the particular combination of lust and financial crimes ("Wert not for gold and women; there would be no damnation . . . ," II. i. 278). Other not unexpected satiric themes include social pretence ("Great men were Gods, if beggers could not kill e'm," II. ii. 106), political irresponsibility, ambition and the like.

One sin which is decried with unusual rigor is that of artificial face-painting, cosmetics. In the best known speech of the play, Vindice muses on the skull of his dead mistress, and observes:

> Do's the Silke-worme expend her yellow labours
> For thee? for thee dos she undoe herselfe?
> Are Lord-ships sold to maintaine Lady-ships
> For the poore benefit of a bewitching minute?
>
> (III. v. 75–78)

> Dos every proud and selfe-affecting Dame
> Camphire her face for this? and grieve her Maker
> In sinfull baths of milke,—when many an infant starves,
> For her superfluous out-side, all for this?
>
> (III. v. 87–90)

The condemnation of gilding the surface is not as superficial as it may seem to the contemporary reader of the play (or of the other Renaissance works which feature this same theme). This particular cosmetic duplicity assumes the status of a symbolic sin for Tourneur and other Jacobean satirists. It is the epitome of artifice in its worst sense, opposed to nature. And for Tourneur, it is even more. The juxtaposition of a "superfluous out-side" with "this"—the skull—dominates the play. Eliot thought that Webster saw the skull beneath the skin, but it is Tourneur who is the master of this vision. The skull—literally, the skull of the dead Gloriana—is the central image of the play. It is echoed in the play's multiple references to the forehead. Over and over, this part of the body is brought to our attention: "Strike thou my fore-head into dauntless Marble . . . " (I. iii. 9); "Ile kill him in his fore-head, hate there feede . . . " (I. ii. 123); "Throwne inck upon the fore-head of our state . . ." (I. ii. 4); "Sufficient in himselfe to make your fore-head/ Dazzle the world with Jewels . . ." (II. i. 212–13). Each time the forehead is mentioned, we are reminded of the skull beneath it. This skull-forehead pattern of imagery, like so much else in *The Revenger's Tragedy,* is in kind conventional but in quantity unusual. Many of Tourneur's contemporaries utilize the symbology, but few use it as often or as effectively. It is an important emblem of the range of Tourneur's satiric vision.

To understand the contemporaneity of such satire, we must go back for a moment to our discussion of the setting of Tourneur's tragedy. We have already remarked that the degenerate Italian court was seen by Renaissance Englishmen as a symbolic focal point of all possible sins. But it is equally true that the Italianate scene was not meant to be taken strictly as an exotic and removed locus. On the contrary, the mythical and Machiavellian world of the Englishman's Italy was often "a purely conventional backcloth for English characters and manners."[19] In 1601, for example, Ben Jonson's *Every Man in his Humour*, a play noted for its biting and effective satire, was published in a quarto edition, with the action of the play set in Florence, and a cast of such Italianate characters as Lorenzo Senior, Prospero, Thorello, Stephano, and the like. In the 1616 folio edition of the same play, the scene is London, and the above characters have changed their names to Kno'well, Kitely, and Stephan. Clearly, the satirist, who wishes to denounce his own society and yet to earn his living pleasing members of that society, is well advised to disguise, at least thinly, the object of his satiric barbs. At the same time, if he wishes to make his point at all, this disguising cannot be so convincing as to really hide his target. Hence, a conventional and mythologized Italy becomes to the satirist what "Arcadia" was to his pastoralist kin. It is a literary setting that enables the author to deal with English society without insulting Englishmen, and at the same time fools no one.

If Tourneur's Italy is, then, England, what specific English vices does *The Revenger's Tragedy* scourge? Superficially, of course, the same sins which damn the Italian court of the play: lust, usury, human justice elevated over divine vengeance, cosmetics, and the like. As symbolized by the skull-forehead motif, however, it seems that these specific social flaws are consumed under a more general satiric target, that of a transformed society. As Murray notes,

The play depicts a world of inverted values, a dark world in which torchlight makes an "artificial noone" for scenes of evil (I. iv. 33), and there is always a sense that the "day is out ath-socket,/ That it is Noone at Mid-night (II. ii. 257–258). People disguise themselves and dissemble their true intentions, and their expectations are transformed by ironic reversals in action and word. Transforming puns, metaphors and personifications are everywhere.[20]

The particular vices upon which Tourneur focuses, then, are symptomatic of a larger transformation, in which the entire moral order of the society is toppling. As a number of commentators have pointed out, this is precisely what a great many Jacobean English authors thought was happening to their country under James. According to J. W. Lever,

. . . the serious playwrights of the age were aware of a wider transformation of society taking place throughout Europe and undermining all traditional human relationships. It consisted in the growth and concentration of state power, the destruction of the Italian city republics, the conversion of English, French, and Spanish noblemen into court parasites, the absorption of petty despotisms by great monarchies, and the concomitant suppression of a wide range of individual freedoms.[21]

Interestingly, the author of this quotation is not specifically speaking of Tourneur, yet is drawn to the specific word, "transformation," which, as we have noted several times, characterizes Tourneur's satire. *The Revenger's Tragedy* is "distanced" from Jacobean England by both a series of literary medievalisms and its Italian setting. Nevertheless, it becomes clear that one of the things the play is "about" is Tourneur's "here and now." When Vindice is told that Lussurioso wants a pander, he resolves,

> And therefore ile put on that knave for once,
> And be a right man then, *a man a'th Time*,
> For to be honest is not to be ith world . . . .
> (I. i. 100–102; italics mine)

It seems doubtful that Tourneur's audience would think that Vindice's "Time" was not the present. The play, writes Lever,

. . . is acutely responsive to the contemporary scene. Italy as the cradle of despotism may be left in the shadows, but Jacobean England makes up a lurid picture of waste and corruption, in which wealth and fertility are being squandered away by spendthrift heirs, the new rich, and noblemen turned courtiers. Patrimonies are "washed a-pieces," "fruitfields turned into bastards." Estates are sold to pay for the fantastic extravagance of court dress.

. . . Usurers flourish, while the common people are ruined by the endless processes of the law.[22]

The skull and the forehead of *The Revenger's Tragedy* are the
emblems of a gaudy exterior masking a moribund interior, of illusion
and artifice disguising a reality and a nature which have been transformed into a hollow-eyed and gaping spectre. Tourneur's work is a
bitter and fully committed satiric portrait of the waste and corruption of an England ruled by a slobbering invert, stumbling into what
we would call the modern world, but to Tourneur looked like hell.
The skull and forehead imagery of the play does, however, go
beyond Jacobean satire. It does not simply suggest the transformation and reversal of a contemporary social scheme, but is equally
suggestive of a more specific "philosophical" or perhaps "theological" bias of Tourneur's satire. This bias takes us back again to Tourneur the conservative, with moral and literary roots in the Middle
Ages and "primitive Christianity."[23] With its "grimly mocking
treatment of death," and its "macabre mood," *The Revenger's
Tragedy* recaptures the spirit of "one particular kind of moral
emblem, perhaps one of the most powerful and pervasive of all in
medieval and Renaissance art, the Dance of Death."[24] Through his
constant iteration of the morbid imagery of the skull, Tourneur
"tells a timeless parable of man's wickedness and God's punishment
for sin."[25] The Dance of Death motif, unlike the medieval morality
play influence, suggests that Tourneur's characters are not so much
choosing between allegorized virtues and vices, but playing out on
this earth a grim comedy, in which Death writes the script and
everyone is ultimately a loser.

There is, then, a sense in which this *Danse Macabre* motif may be
seen as clashing with the play's morality motif. Does man choose a
life of vice or virtue, or is he merely the puppet of an allegorical
skeleton? Actually, this conflict seems less paradoxical within a balanced historical perspective. It must be remembered that *The Revenger's Tragedy* was written in an age in which Protestants and
Catholics were still clashing throughout Europe on this and similar
questions. That both strains exist in this work results not so much in
a theological contradiction as in a dramatic tension. Tourneur may
be   flawed   as   a   philosopher,   but   the   relationship   between
philosophical themes of free will and determination in his plays
reflects contradictions of tragic dimension in the world around him.

In effect, we can never be certain if Vindice is a conscious sinner, tempted into the ways of Lussurioso, the Duke and their nest of vices, or if he is simply one more helpless citizen in a damned world. This ambiguity, far from confusing the issue, seems to make Vindice a more interesting and engaging character. In an age when determinism has passed from the theologians to the psychologists, Vindice's relations with the forces ordering his world are significant, because they parallel so closely our own ambiguities in this area.

It is perhaps simpler, but equally productive, to see the skull of *The Revenger's Tragedy* not as presiding over a Dance of Death but as a *memento mori*, a reminder that the end of life is death. Such reminders, inherited by Renaissance English culture from the Middle Ages, remained quite popular in Tourneur's day. Other artists see the skull much as Tourneur has Vindice see it, as an emblem of the futility of earthly preoccupations. He remarks of Gloriana's skull:

> . . . is not he absurd,
> Whose fortunes are upon their faces set,
> That feare no other God but winde and wet?
>
> (III. 5. 66–68)

> Here might a scornefull and ambitious woman
> Lookd through and through her selfe,—see Ladies with false formes
> You deceive men, but cannot deceive wormes.
>
> (III. 5. 99–101)

The earliest English emblem writer, Geoffrey Whitney, in *A Choice of Emblemes*, pictures a skull, under the heading *Ex maximo minimum* ("From the most the least").[26] The verse which accompanies this emblem clearly reveals the tradition with which Tourneur is working:

> Where lively once, Gods image was expreste,
> Wherein, sometime was sacred reason plac'de,
> The head, I meane, that is so ritchly blest,
> With sighte, with smell, with hearinge, and with taste.
> Lo, now a skull, both rotten, bare, and drye,
> A relike meete in charnell house to lye.

The skull as *memento mori* provides a rich context for Tourneur's

Jacobean satire. The transformations of the world of *The Revenger's Tragedy*, representing Tourneur's view of the degeneration of his own culture, are worldly. Vices, like lust, wastefulness, usury, cosmetics, policitical ambition, all are based on a drive to acquire the things of this earth. To Tourneur, these drives are evil not only in and of themselves, not only because they violate natural or human law, but also, and most importantly perhaps, because they transgress a divine order. *Memento mori* functions within that order to remind men that their earthly existence is unimportant in relation to their immortal souls. The play's characters are sinners because they have transposed these two unequal values. Even Vindice's sin fits into this framework—human justice is as earthly a preoccupation as human lust or covetousness. The ultimate vision of Tourneur's satire seems to be that of a social order which has transformed a divine moral order into a squalid and corrupt quest for the things of this world. *The Revenger's Tragedy* asserts that a society which neglects death has forgotten God.

VI *Language*

The complexly interrelated thematic structure of *The Revenger's Tragedy* is presented in an appropriately rich and multidimensional poetic diction. The language of the play is, above all else, explosive. In a play which features several rather long monologues, Tourneur's tone is almost never discursive or reflective. As the play seems to flash from character to character, from theme to theme, so the language is darting, surprising, and quick.

Poetry is built of words (as the Taj Mahal is built of stones), and Tourneur's choice of words is revealing. R. A. Foakes has sampled the vocabulary of the work and finds an overwhelming use of words connected to notions of sin: adultery (used 8 times), rape (6), incest (5), treason (13), false (16), base (14), wrong (11), shame (17), lust or lustful (20), villain and villainous (41), fault (9), knave (15), doom (9), curse (12), damn and damnation (17), hell (18), devil (15). The word sin itself is used thirty times.

Words signifying virtue appear often, but not as often: good (26), virgin or virginity (9), virtue (6), chastity (13). Foakes offers a comparison of words related to death in Tourneur's play and Hamlet, "the tragedy of Shakespeare's in which words relating to death are most prominent: in this the occurrences of die, death, kill, and murder total 77, in *The Revenger's Tragedy*, 129. *Hamlet* is a very much longer play.":[27] Clearly, the satiric and moral preoccupations of the work are reflected in its vocabulary. Indeed, based upon vocabulary alone, a good case could be made for those, like T. S. Eliot, who see Tourneur as pathologically obsessed with evil.

This obsessive vocabulary must, however, be balanced with another, parodistic feature of the language of *The Revenger's Tragedy*, "an insistent note of ludicrous exaggeration:"[28]

> . . . the uprightest man, (if such there be,
> That sinne but seaven times a day). . . .

> (I. i. 26–27)

> Nay and you draw teares once, go you to bed,
> Wet will make yron blush and change to red;
> Brother it raines, twill spoile your dagger, house it.

> (IV. iv. 51–53)

> . . . I have great sins, I must have daies,
> Nay months deere sonne, with penitential heaves,
> To life 'em out. . . .

> (II. ii. 214–16)

> I have beene witnesse
> To the surrenders of a thousand virgins. . . .

> (I. iii. 54–55)

These exaggerated lines speak not for the compulsive moral pessimist, but the careful and controlled artist who parodies such compulsion. The seeming paradox between an obsessive vocabulary and a parodistic hyperbole can be easily reconciled. The words of *The Revenger's Tragedy* are not the words of the play's author, but of his characters. Vindice uses words like sin, lust, evil, damn, and hell very seriously. He also drifts quite unknowingly into ludicrous exaggeration. Usually he fails to realize just how overblown his rhetoric is. It is Vindice whom Tourneur's words prove to be adolescently preoccupied with evil, not Tourneur. It is Vindice's adolescent preoccupations with damnation which leads him into an immature attempt through vengeance to purge his environment, and this action, motivated by an acute sense of sin, leads Vindice himself into sin and, ultimately, damnation.

Tourneur's control of poetic language can also be seen in the use within *The Revenger's Tragedy* of a heavy and consistent use of commonplace moralistic expressions. Again, some students of the play have been confused because they presume when Tourneur's characters come up with an inappropriate moral saw, that Tourneur himself is trying to get across some hackneyed point of conventional morality. Yet, clearly, we are not to think that either Supervacuo or Tourneur believes that ". . . this true reason gathers,/ None can possesse that dispossesse their fathers . . ." (II. ii. 308–9). The point is, of course, that Supervacuo believes just the opposite, and indeed spends most of his time within the play trying as hard as he can to dispossess his father. As R. A. Foakes comments, "The test of such saws, which come thick and fast through much of the dialogue, is their relation to what the characters do. They continually expose the half-relevance of their sayings, or an ironical application to themselves, or a contradiction between words and deeds, in their actions. . . ."[29] Tourneur is not "the most subjective of Elizabethan dramatists."[30] The *sententia* of *The Revenger's Tragedy* are not hysterical attempts to dredge a sentimentalized ethic from an evil universe. Rather, they are a careful and controlled aspect of Tourneur's dissection of that universe, a dissection undertaken in the serious and mature search for a much more profound—albeit medieval—morality.

Tourneur exploits even the crude and hackneyed potential of the English language. The juxtaposition of crude moral platitudes and equally crude immoral actions helps to generate and sustain a keen and discriminating moral perspective for the play's spectators. The subtlest shades of hypocrisy and deceit reveal themselves in the clash between crude words and cruder actions.

The metaphorical structure of the play shows a similar mastery of the dramatic possibilities of poetic language. Tourneur's metaphors in this play are short, compressed, and powerful. They frequently invoke some aspects of the human body, imparting to the language a kind of physicality which both pervades and heightens the entire drama: "I have endur'd you with an eare of fire . . ." (II. i. 258); ". . . I would raise my state upon her brest/ And call her eyes my Tennants . . ." (II. i. 107–8); ". . . discontent and want/ Is the best clay to mould a villain off . . ." (IV. i. 57–58). *The Revenger's Tragedy* is full of these "brief compressed metaphors, hitting one with an almost physical force."[31] Such imagistic language, which "has the rare and sudden quality of inevitable poetry"[32] has several functions within the work.

Least importantly, but perhaps most often noted, Tourneur's poetic language is impressive in and of itself. Critics who find the play a wretched drama, as well as those who admire it, unite in their appreciation of Tourneur's style. Frequently, readers of *The Revenger's Tragedy* have commented on this style with what one critic terms "the flame analogy." There is "the fiery jet of his molten verse," a style which "burns in lines of intense metaphorical concentration."[33] Parrott and Ball twice describe *The Revenger's Tragedy* as "fiery."[34]

In addition to being admirable in and of itself, Tourneur's fiery verse accomplishes several dramatic purposes. His compact, hard-hitting, explosive language invites, even demands, a certain immediacy and emotionality of reaction. The poetry of *The Revenger's Tragedy* seldom attempts to elicit a meditative response. This immediacy complements the satiric functions of the play. In order to follow the moral complexities of the drama unfolding rapidly before them, the audience must react very quickly to the play's characters and action. Tourneur's explosive, quick, and physical images provoke just such a reaction. In effect, they suggest to the viewer or reader what his reactions should be, and simultaneously engage his emotions in those reactions.

Moreover, a language which prompts an immediate and powerful reaction serves as a unifying effect on a play which is both complex and multidimensional. We have seen the multiple influences and sources at work in this play, and it is Tourneur's language which brings together and vivifies what could otherwise be a kind of anthology. By creating, guiding, and intensifying our reactions to the world of *The Revenger's Tragedy*, the language of the play turns what could have been a mishmash of Renaissance and medieval theatrical and moral traditions into an engaging and coherent mosaic.

The vocabulary, *sententia*, and imagery of this work are the product of craftsmanship and careful utilization of the media of the poetic drama. Tourneur's handling of these poetic tools is striking as poetry and impressively functional as theater. The language of *The Revenger's Tragedy* fulfills the implied double goals of dramatic poetry: it is poetic and it is dramatic.

VII   The Revenger's Tragedy *in Context*

A consideration of Tourneur's best and best known work leads, by one route or another, to the rest of Tourneur's works, either to show how different this work is from the others, or to show how much it is the same. It seems to this writer that the similarities far outweigh the differences. *The Revenger's Tragedy* can be seen as both a reworking and a progression from *The Transformed Metamorphosis* and *Laugh and Lie Down*. That it is also an introduction to Tourneur's later works will be clear when those works are considered.

In both the early works satire plays an important role. Both depict a fallen world (*The Transformed Metamorphosis* somewhat more complexly and subtly) of similar configurations. This similarity of course extends neatly to Vindice and his world. For example, one target of the satire of *The Transformed Metamorphosis* is lust, in particular, lust in old men. The vice is to Tourneur the epitome of wasteful sin:

> O, that old age (that kept the tresuries
> Of great Apollo once), whose faltring tongue,
> Intreates old earth performe his obsequies,
> Should now by hell be metamorphosde yong,
> And with desire of soule-infecting dong,
> Seeke unto vice, weake infancie to winne,
> And make his heart, Epithesis of sinne.
>
> (ll. 232–38)

This picture of aged desire seems not too distantly related to one of the fools in *Laugh and Lie Down:*

Now, next her, sat a man, well stept in yeeres, but fine in apparrell, and so briske in countenance, as if he had fed upon an Elixar, then in body, to preserve the smoothnesse of his countnance, to deceive the sight of a simple Eie, fedde onely uppon a Snayle, and so litle at once that he kept an exceeding spare diet: which, not being wholesome for all complexions, I meant not to meddle with. . . .

(ll. 452–58)

Clearly, both these venial geriatrics are prototypes of the Duke in *The Revenger's Tragedy,* that "gray hayrd adultery" (I. i. 1), who describes himself in terms easily transposed into *The Transformed Metamorphosis:*

> It well becomes that Judge to nod at crimes,
> That dos commit greater himselfe and lives:
> I may forgive a disobedient error,
> That expect pardon for adultery
> And in my old daies am a youth in lust:
> Many a beauty have I turnd to poyson
> In the deniall, covetous of all,
> Age hot, is like a Monster to be seene:
> My haires are white, and yet my sinnes are Greene.
>
> (II. ii. 352–60)

The fallen worlds of all three works show other specific correspondences. The wasting away of patrimonies, for example, plays an unusually important role in each. In each work, the society satirized is exotic, overtly foreign—the unnamed dream island of *Laugh and Lie Down*; Delta in *The Transformed Metamorphosis*; and Italy in *The Revenger's Tragedy*. Yet, clearly, each of these corrupt societies represents England, with its contemporary vices and failings. Finally, though, the fallen world of Tourneur's works is the entire world, the world that fell with Adam. All of Tourneur's works discussed thus far are set within the environs of a corrupted and sinful earth. It is a world which is "transformed," a metaphor which is clearly communicated in both *The Transformed Metamorphosis* and *The Revenger's Tragedy* in images of day and night, darkness and light: "Why is the skie so pitchie then at noone,/ As though the day were govern'd by the Moone?" (*The Transformed Metamorphosis*, Prologue, 34–35); ". . . is the day out ath-socket/That it is Noone at Mid-night?" (*The Revenger's Tragedy*; II. ii. 256–57).

What, Tourneur asks, is to be done in and about such a world? What specifically, can man or a man do to reverse this corruption? As we have seen, this problem is the central thematic concern of *The Transformed Metamorphosis*. In that poem, the world is redeemed—retransformed or metamorphosed—through the agency of Mavortio. In a sense, however, Mavortio does not really solve the problems posed by the worlds of these first three works. Mavortio, it must be remembered, is a very God-like man (or a very man-like God, depending upon one's reading of the poem). Although he is a "knight" with a squire, riding on a horse, bleeding, becoming tired, and the like, he is also the child of the muses who has left his heavenly home to solve the problems of Delta. One feels that through his dual nature, Mavortio evades a solution by negating the problem of mankind in a lost world. Tourneur seems uncertain as to whether the problems of the fallen society can be solved by an extraordinary man, or only by a compassionate descendent God. Still, in this early work, Tourneur raises the question of redemption or salvation for a sinful cosmos. This question will dominate most of his other works.

The Revenger's Tragedy raises the same redemptive themes, but deals with them in a way which is at once less simpleminded and less confusing. It is a study of one wrong solution to the problems of fallen humankind. Vindice, in effect, assumes that Mavortio was a man, and if Mavortio can purge the world of evil, so can he. The times are out of joint, and fully cursing the spite, Vindice intends to set them right. Throughout the play, Vindice wrongly interprets his personal revenge as a large purgative which shall cleanse his society: "Let our hid flames breake out, as fire, as lightning/ To blast this villanous Dukedome vext with sinne . . ." (I. ii. 4–5; note the image).

The Revenger's Tragedy is the tragedy of the revenger, because it chronicles the ultimate irony of human justice. By attacking sinners, the revenger thinks he can eliminate sin, yet his attack is itself sinful. Mavortio may be a symbolic Christ, but Vindice simply tries to play Christ, and, of course, fails. The salvation of the fallen world cannot be effected by a Vindice who holds up a skull to make us see death, but only by "that eternall eye/ That see's through flesh and all" (I. iii. 74–75). In this play, Tourneur goes back over the ground of *The Transformed Metamorphosis* and resolves that poem's central ambiguity: it says that Mavortio cannot be a man, and a man cannot be a Mavortio. In this sense, of course, the tragedy is not simply that of the revenger, but of all mankind. Man, a weak, blind, and sinful creature, inhabitant of a sinful world, can do nothing to purge that world of its sin without corrupting himself further. The only salvation will come from God, while the only human comfort will come from faith in divine justice. Without that faith, the world can finally seem nothing more than "plagues, confusions, darkness, devils" (I. vi. 100–103)—but that is *The Atheist's Tragedy*.

CHAPTER 5

The Atheist's Tragedy

ALTHOUGH *The Atheist's Tragedy*, like *The Revenger's Tragedy*, is in many ways a composite of theatrical and literary traditions, the central structuring principle of the later work is allegorical. While irony, satire, diction, and a wide variety of dramatic and poetic conventions all contribute to the ultimate effect of the drama, these elements are largely ornamentation on a skeleton of symbolic characters engaged in symbolic actions. We shall, therefore, approach Tourneur's last extent play first through its plot and characters, consider the themes and meaning of the work, and conclude with a brief look at the way in which Tourneur marshals the available resources of the Jacobean dramatist to illuminate those themes.

I *Plot*

Since *The Atheist's Tragedy* is generally considered the lesser of Tourneur's plays and is not read as frequently as *The Revenger's Tragedy*, it is possible that some readers are not familiar with the work. For such readers it is necessary to note that what follows is even more inadequate than the usual plot summary—for a very simple reason. The action of this play is, by any standard tinged with a realistic or naturalistic bias, outrageous. It is a plot which makes *Everyman* look like Ibsen by comparison. Naturally, such a plot becomes even more outrageous when condensed. It is, however, clear that this outrageousness was intended. In fact, it is absolutely necessary to the meaning of *The Atheist's Tragedy*—which stands finally as a most carefully constructed drama—that the action of the play depends upon what at first appears wild coincidence, totally inadequate motivation and blatant theatricality.

The play begins with a brief discussion of the philosophy of nature between D'amville, the atheist, and Borachio, his "instrument," or accomplice:

> D'AMVILLE: Borachio, thou art read
> In Nature and her large Philosophie.
> Observ'st thou not the very selfe same course
> Of revolution both in Man and Beast?
> BORACHIO: The same. For birth, growth,
> state, decay and death. . . .
>
> (I. i. 6–10)

These two encourage young Charlemont (the "Honest Man" of the subtitle) in his plan to "set forward to the warre" (I. i. 71), against the wishes of Baron Montferrers, Charlemont's father (and D'amville's brother). Charlemont, aided by a gift of one thousand crowns from D'amville, does leave, after winning his father's permission and taking leave of the chaste Castabella, his sweetheart, whom he leaves in the safekeeping of Languebeau Snuffe, a self-made Puritan clergyman~who "will be a testamonie to the integritie of your promises" (I. ii. 110–11). As soon as Charlemont leaves, D'amville bribes Snuffe to help lure Castabella into a marriage with D'amville's sickly son Roussard. Castabella's mother, a woman of extremely lustful appetites named Levidulcia, also attempts to promote this marriage, arguing on the basis of her own example that the way to convince a woman is "not through her reason, but her blood" (I. iv. 67–68). Belforest, Castabella's father, insists on the marriage, and only Sebastian, D'amville's other son, objects, crying "A rape, a rape, a rape!" (I. iv. 137).

Act 2 begins at a banquet following the forced wedding, during which D'amville has arranged for the disguised Borachio to give a false report of Charlemont's death at Ostend (thus leaving D'amville the clear and sole heir to Montferrers). The atheist encourages the servants to become drunk and then, while guiding Montferrers home, pushes him into a pit where he is killed by Borachio. Meanwhile, Roussard confesses himself too sickly to act the part of a new husband: "Thou shalt not lose thy maidenhead too night" (II. iii. 38). Thoughts of wedding nights, however, arouse Levidulcia who entices and arranges an assignation with Sebastian.

D'amville gloats over the progress of his plots:

> Not any circumstance
> That stood within the reach of the designe
> Of persons, dispositions, matter, time

> Or place, but by this brain of mine was made
> An Instrumentall help. . . .
>
> (II. iv. 122–26)

He is not at all put off by an immediate display of "Thunder and Lightning" (s.d. II. iv. 162). Meanwhile, Levidulcia, admitting "I could clasp with any man" (II. iii. 77), is about to clasp with Fresco, a clownish servant, when Sebastian arrives. Fresco hides, Levidulcia entertains Sebastian, but Belforest makes his appearance. Levidulcia extricates herself from this rather compromising situation by having Sebastian pretend he has chased Fresco off the street and into her room.

On the battlefield, the ghost of Montferrers comes to Charlemont telling of his death and urging Charlemont to return home to: "Attend with patience the sucesse of things, But leave revenge unto the King of kings" (II. vi. 26–27).

At the beginning of Act 3, D'amville presides over the double funerals of Montferrers and the supposedly dead Charlemont. Charlemont, however, returns to find Castabella at his tomb. She tells him of her forced marriage. Charlemont confronts D'amville and Sebastian, and begins to fight with the latter, when the ghost of his father returns and again bids him:

> Hold, Charlemont!
> Let him revenge my murder, and thy wrongs
> To whom the Justice of Revenge belongs.
>
> (III. ii. 45–47)

D'amville has Charlemont arrested, and gives Sebastian one thousand crowns for fighting Charlemont. Sebastian, however, knows that his foe could have killed him but refrained. He uses the money to free Charlemont. D'amville feigns reconciliation with his nephew who, in turn, freely forgives his uncle.

In Act 4, the plot so thickens as to congeal. Most of the act is an overt and macabre dance of and with death. It begins with two assignations at a bawdy house near the Church of St. Winifrid. Here, Sebastian meets Levidulcia, and Snuffe offers himself to one Soquette. Meanwhile D'amville sends Borachio to ambush Charlemont as he walks in the graveyard of the church, meditating on his

father's death. Realizing that Roussard is unable to make love to
Castabella, and fearful that his line will die out, D'amville resolves
to rape his daughter-in-law Castabella. In the churchyard,
Borachio's ambush fails, and in the ensuing fight he is killed by
Charlemont. In the same churchyard, Snuffe and Soquette prepare
to make love, Snuffe disguising himself "for securitie sake" (IV. ii.
63). But Charlemont surprises them and they flee, leaving the disguise which Charlemont assumes just in time to frighten off D'amville as he attempts to rape Castabella. Charlemont and Castabella,
reunited, happily fall asleep amid the tombs. Snuffe returns and
discovers the dead Borachio, whom he at first confuses with
Soquette and to whom—which?—he makes lewd advances. D'amville returns and has Charlemont arrested for the killing of Borachio.

Meanwhile, Belforest discovers his wife's infidelity with Sebastian, catches the adulterous lovers at the bawdy house, where the
rivals fight and ultimately kill each other. When Levidulcia sees the
carnage she repents: "Heere I behold the hatefulnesse of lust . . ."
(IV. v. 70), and kills herself.

This brings us to the final act, which begins with a highly conventional scene in which D'amville is seen counting and gloating over
his gold. He is informed of the death of his son Sebastian in the
duel, which is immediately followed by the death of his other son,
Roussard, succumbing at last to his illnesses. The distracted D'amville, all dynastic ambitions foiled, goes to the trial of Charlemont,
where he is to be one of the judges. After disposing of some of the
play's minor characters, the judges sentence Charlemont to death
for the murder of Borachio. Castabella leaps up to the scaffold to join
him cheerfully in death:

> . . . we in vertue are the best for Death,
> While yet we have not liv'd to such an age,
> That the encrusting canker of our sinnes
> Hath spread too farre upon us.
>
> (V. ii. 152–55)

D'amville, even more distracted by the calm of the two condemned
lovers, tries to discover the source of their bliss in the face of death.
Charlemont tells him that "the peace of conscience arises in it selfe"
(V. ii. 177), which does not seem to be much help to D'amville. He
then insists on beheading his nephew himself but, *"As he raises up*

the Axe, strikes out his owne braines" (s.d. V. II. 177). Charlemont and Castabella are instantly acquitted and inherit the titles of Belforest, D'amville, and Montferrers. The play closes as Charlemont pronounces that *"Patience is the honest mans revenge"* (V. ii. 303).

II *Character*

Clearly, such a plot does not call for the creation of characters who manifest anything resembling psychological realism. Indeed, *The Atheist's Tragedy* would be crippled by such characters, or by a performance which attempted to create an atmosphere of "believability." It is probably impossible to "motivate" a character to knock out his own brains accidentally. The inhabitants of the world Tourneur created for this play were never meant to be confused with real people.

What then are these characters? They are symbols, personifications of ideas: Each major character in the play bodies forth some very specific attitude toward human life and the world in which it exists. These attitudes are carefully balanced within the structure of the play for purposes of explication, comparison, and judgment. The cast, in short, is composed of "embodied principles or ideas."[1]

It is very easy to mistake this formulation for a simple mishandling of dramatic materials. If *The Atheist's Tragedy* is compared to most other dramas—Renaissance or non-Renaissance—it may seem an expression of "a naive and at times quite crude theatricalism."[2] It is not. It is only naive and crude according to standards which it never attempts to meet. What the play lacks in human complexity it makes up for in thematic sophistication. As we shall see, simplistic characters can be arranged and manipulated complexly. Allardyce Nicoll has wisely noted: "we are in a world of art and not in the world of naturalism. The strange and the impossible may be used to serve the purposes of the shaping imagination."[3] In this case, the "shaping imagination" is interested in ideas—ideas which have a profound relation to "real" human life, but ideas nonetheless, not people.

The full title of the play hints at a parallelism of both plot and character: *The Atheist's Tragedy or The Honest Man's Revenge.* Thus the work features two main groups of characters, the "atheists" and the "honest men", with each group consisting of a primary character and several secondary characters in a balanced and complex interrelationship. The plot consists of the failure of the atheists and the success of the honest men. Since the atheists are the active agents of the play ("patience" being the honest man's revenge) they are the more interesting characters and it is to them that we now turn.

The principal atheist of the play is, of course, D'amville, *the* atheist of the title. Since Tourneur wishes to make very clear the major antagonistic position of the drama, D'amville is a talkative character with a philosophical bent, and Borachio plays the role of intellectual "yes man" to whom he may explain his philosophy. D'amville's "atheism" is both atheism in general and a rather particular class of atheism (as, say, Everyman is both all men and a particular version of all men). He is "the archetypal Renaissance atheist synthesized from contemporary opinion."[4] According to such opinion, the atheist is, by definition, a complete and unredeemable villain who was equally feared and loathed by all men of piety and/or sense, since in rejecting God he has rejected the only source of ethics and morality in the universe. Because an atheist neither believed in, nor feared, God, he or she naturally also neither believed in nor feared God's retribution for sin and the punishment of eternal damnation. All actions, then, are judged only by the effects produced in this world. Most Jacobeans realized that within a strictly worldly context, sin sometimes is much more rewarding than virtue. The atheist was thus, by definition, committed to a life of evil. That the entire action of the play asserts that divine retribution does in fact exist is only one of the major ironies of *The Atheist's Tragedy*. D'amville's negative freedom from religious ethics is signaled even in his name: "This appears to combine the English 'vile' with the French 'D'ame' to mean 'of evil spirit.' In 'damn' is an indication of the villain's fate."[5]

To the Elizabethans, however, atheism was not simply a negative philosophy. The atheist not only did not believe in God, he did believe in an anti-Christian set of substitute values, and it is through his beliefs that D'amville particularizes himself.

First and foremost, D'amville believes in "Nature and her large Philosophie" (I. i. 7). This is not the goddess Natura, but simply nature. What "honestmen" attribute to "some power above Her [nature] that controules her force" (V. i. 126–27), D'amville considers simply a mechanistic phenomenon. Thus, immediately after the murder of his brother, D'amville mocks:

> That power of rule Philosophers ascribe
> To him they call the supreame of the Starres:

> Making their influences governours
> Of Sublunarie Creatures; when their selves
> Are senselesse of their operations.
>
> (II. iv. 157–61)

At this point there is a most blatant warning from the "supreame of the Starres," a display of thunder and lightning at which éven the villainous Borachio cringes. D'amville, however, has a "natural" explanation:

> What!
> Doest start at thunder? Credit my believe,
> T'is a meere effect of nature. An
> Exhalation hot and dry, involv'd
> Within a watrie vapour i' the middle
> Region of the ayre.
>
> (II. iv. 7–12)

D'amville substitutes for God a concept of "nature" uncontrolled by any intelligence or moral force. From this premise come several conclusions. The most obvious of these is that man is but an animal. Mankind follows (to use the language of Act 1, scene 1) the selfsame course of revolution through birth, growth, state, decay, and death as the beasts. D'amville substitutes for what a prudent Elizabethan Englishman would term a "natural" belief in God, a proud, self-assertive and "unnatural" belief in nature.

Surprisingly, D'amville does not seem to presume that man's animality is an invitation to a life of sensualism and lust. In this respect he differs sharply from the conventional Renaissance atheist. As we shall see, this characteristic has been reserved for Levidulcia. Tourneur is making a sharp division between the atheists who rely upon the senses and those who place faith in reason. Indeed, D'amville's one truly sensualist act, the attempted rape of Castabella, is committed not for sensual but for almost comically rational reasons: D'amville does not wish to have fun, he wishes to have heirs, and since his own sons seem incapable of continuing his line, he undertakes the task himself. Murray· notes the wit of the encounter: "Poor D'amville cannot even make Castabella understand what he intends, and as the scene continues it becomes plain that if he triumphs, she will be the first woman ever to be raped by the instrument of a man's reason."[6]

If the belief that man is just another animal does not turn D'amville into a raging sensualist, it does nevertheless have grave and, literally, damnable consequences. Since D'amville believes that human life, like animal life, ends with death, the twinned and related Christian goals of a virtuous life on earth and a heavenly reward are both negated. The atheist substitutes similar twinned and related goals, the acquisition of material wealth (and its accompanying power) while he lives, and the founding of a dynasty which will constitute a sort of earthly hereafter when he is dead.

D'amville's materialism is highly stylized. It reaches its epitome in the opening scene of Act 5, in which Tourneur presents, almost casually, a familiar emblem of the worldly materialist: "Musicke. A clozet discover'd. A servant sleeping with lights and money before him. Enter D'amville (s.d. V. i. 1–3)." D'amville "handles the gold" and exclaims:

> Heere sounds a musicke whose melodious touch,
> Like Angels voices ravishes the sense.
> Behold thou ignorant Astronomer,
> Whose wandring speculation seeks among
> The planets for mens fortunes! with amazement
> Behold thine errour and be planet-strucke.
> These are the Starres whose operations make
> The fortunes and the destinies of men.
> Yond' lesser eyes of heav'n (Like Subjects rais'd
> Into their loftie houses, when their Prince
> Rides underneath th'ambition of their loves)
> Are mounted onely to behold the face,
> Of your more rich imperious eminence,
> With unprevented sight.[7]
>
> (V. i. 16–29)

While this speech fits the character and situation very nicely (for example, the ironic contrasting pun involving "Angels" as ministers of God and the coin of the same name in line 17), it is by no means original. In the first scene of Jonson's *Volpone* (1605) a servant of the worldly, materialistic hero "withdraws the curtain, and discovers piles of gold, plate, jewels, &c." (s.d. I. i. 3). and Volpone exclaims, in language strikingly like that of D'amville,

> Hail the world's soul, and mine! more glad than is
> The teeming earth to see the longed-for sun

> Peep through the horns of the celestial Ram,
> Am I to view thy splendour darkening his;
> That lying here, amongst my other hoards,
> Show'st like a flame by night, or like the day
> Struck out of chaos, when all darkness fled
> Unto the centre.
>
> (I. i. 3–10)

Unlike conventional atheists D'amville does not simply ignore the future. Where Marlowe's Faustus is willing to sign away his immortal soul for twenty-four years of earthly power and riches because "I think hell's a fable" (II. i. 125), D'amville is quite concerned with survival after death. Like Faustus, however, D'amville does not believe in heavenly reward or hellish punishment. Rather, D'amville's notion of immortality is tied directly to his progeny. He wishes to become the founder of a great house, a powerful and enduring family. Not surprisingly, one of the chief images of the play is that of the building and destruction of a house, a natural symbol of family fortunes. D'amville is quite explicit about his dynastic ambitions:

> But let me call my projects to accompt,
> For what effect and end I have engag'd
> My selfe in all this bloud? To leave a state
> To the succession of my proper bloud.
>
> (IV. ii. 35–38)

(Note the ironic effect of the pun in these lines: "bloud" ties together D'amville's hopes and his crimes.) It is another of the major ironies of *The Atheist's Tragedy* that the main character's most profound desire and guiding ambition are for the achievement of some sort of immortality. Yet immortality is precisely what Tourneur thinks D'amville has lost even as he searches for it. For D'amville searches in the wrong places—nature and the world encompassed by man's senses—and with the wrong instrument—fallible human reason, unilluminated by faith.

At times D'amville's rational and materialistic attempts to achieve earthly success do not seem so much the medieval horror of "atheism" as a much more modern malady. Peter Murray describes D'amville as almost as much of a "puritan" as an atheist, citing his "materialism" and "industry"; to Robert Ornstein, D'amville is

Tourneur's protest "against superfluity and economic opportunism":
"D'amville's materialism is that of a New Man, a Jacobean parvenu
with a criminal appetite for wealth and status . . . [characterized
by] his moneylending, his mercantile vocabulary, his equation of
material success and providential aid, and his deification of 'industry.' . . ."8

There are moments in the play when it seems D'amville would be
more at home in the corporate boardroom than at a black mass. But
while D'amville is a supremely rationalistic criminal, he is nonetheless a criminal, not an Elizabethan in a grey flannel suit. His
rationalism leads him into fratricide, incest, madness, and death.
D'amville is, is sum, an atheist. His belief in the ultimate power of
his own mind is based upon a disbelief in any supreme power, a
disbelief which Tourneur goes out of his way to prove tragically
misguided. He is not a monster of sensuality, as is Levidulcia, but
an even greater horror, a monster of reason.

Levidulcia more than makes up for what D'amville lacks in sensualism. Her name, like many in the play, clearly points to her one
dimensional nature: Levi-dulcia—"light and sweet." Where D'amville is a complex stereotype, Levidulcia seems even more stylized
than a figure in a morality play. Indeed, she is reminiscent of nothing so much as one of the emblems of the seven deadly sins so
frequently paraded before medieval and early Renaissance audi-
ences and readers (for example, in Spenser and Marlowe). At least
until her hasty conversion and suicide, she is nothing more than a
personification of mindless sexual passion. Even to the modern
reader used to fairly explicit literary treatments of the sexual drive,
there is something almost embarassing about Levidulcia's single-
minded sexuality. Her first lines give some indication of the future
direction of her actions: she enters, with Belforest, as Charlemont is
gently kissing Castabella good-bye (chaperoned by Snuffe—a quite
innocent scene). Her reaction is typical:

> Levidulcia: O ! Heer's your daughter under her servants lips.
> CHARLEMONT: Madame, there is no cause you should mistrust
> The kisse I gave, t'was but a parting one.
> LEVIDULCIA: A lustie bloud! Now by the lip of love
> Were I to choose, your joyning one for mee.
>
> (I. ii. 130–34)

Surely the expression "under her servants lips" has a more carnal
implication than the chaste kiss warrants, and the implication is

made explicit with Levidulcia's wordplay on "parting-joyning" (the latter word having the obvious and accepted slang meaning of sexual intercourse). Like D'amville, Levidulcia sees "nature" as cause and justification for her actions:

> Wise nature (therefore) hath
> Reserv'd for an inducement to our sence,
> Our greatest pleasure in that greatest worke [procreation].
>
> (I. iv. 94–96)

The subplot of *The Atheist's Tragedy* is initiated by Levidulcia's sexual arousal on the wedding might of Castabella and Roussard when

> my affection even with their cold blouds
> (As snow rub'd through an active hand, does make
> The flesh to burne) by agitation is
> Inflamed. I could imbrace, and entertaine
> The ayre to coole it.
>
> (II. iii. 50–54)

Levidulcia's attempts to cool her inflamed flesh, first with Sebastian, then with Fresco, plunges her into the farcical bedroom escapades which emphasize the ridiculousness and total lack of human dignity which is the end of such indiscriminate lust. As a reult of the bloody duel which follows the exposure of this affair, Levidulcia repents and kills herself.

Tourneur's second atheist is an interesting foil to his other characters. Clearly she represents a contrast to D'amville within the camp of the atheists—"the division between the rationalist and the sensualist atheists."[9] Equally clearly, her animalistic view of human love contrasts sharply with the chaste affection of Charlemont and, especially, Castabella. As we shall see later, she also shares with Sebastian an impulsiveness and a complete trust in sensual first impressions.

An equally interesting comparison may be made between Levidulcia and Gratiana of *The Revenger's Tragedy*. Both are mothers of daughters whose very names—Castiza and Castabella— are emblems of chastity. Both attempt to persuade their daughters to sacrifice their virginity for worldly advancement, in both cases to the sons of the plays' chief villains (Roussard, son of D'amville;

Lussurioso, son of the Duke). Both are unsuccessful; and both undergo a surprisingly quick conversion when confronted with their deeds from a new perspective. If the "vices" are easily distinguished in *The Atheist's Tragedy*, the "virtues" tend to cluster together. Thus, while D'amville and Levidulcia seem an almost schematic division of atheism, Charlemont and Castabella represent a unified opposition. This configuration may be presumed to be no accident, in that it serves to demonstrate the unifying effect of virtuous love as contrasted to the isolation of the naturalists. In any event, Charlemont and Castabella can conveniently be discussed together.

Tourneur shares with other writers in the Christian tradition a problem with virtue, a problem which is painfully clear in the characterization of Charlemont and Castabella. Since evil rebels against the divine and moral order of the universe, it tends to be an active force. Since good—in the Christian scheme—submits to this order, it is more often passive. Sadly, for the moralists, active agents in literary works are usually more interesting than passive ones. Nowhere is this more true than in *The Atheist's Tragedy*. Although Charlemont and Castabella are universally understood to be Tourneur's exempla of ideal human beings, there is not too much to say about them: Charlemont is "a cold and unsympathetic figure, but a model of Christian stoicism, carefully designed to point the moral."[10] Tourneur faces the problem of how to write a play about a protagonist whose chief action will be to take no action. If "patience is the honest man's revenge," to watch someone being patient is hardly thrilling.

Tourneur seems aware of this problem, and in the development of his two "honest" characters tries to deal with it. The first and most direct solution Tourneur offers is simply to keep his "main" characters off stage as much as possible. Charlemont spends a large part of the play off at the wars or (twice) locked up in jail. This solution leads to another, related device. If the central models of ideal virtue are limited in their ability to initiate action, they may at any rate be acted upon by their antagonists. This is clearly the direction of melodrama and pathos, but it is a direction in which Tourneur is willing to go. Castabella "acts" by actively resisting the advances of both Roussard and D'amville. Charlemont is persecuted, followed, ambushed, harrassed, jailed, tried, sentenced to execution, and almost executed.

Benign neglect and pathetic persecution are negative solutions to the problems posed by inactive virtue. Happily, Tourneur also attempts a more positive scheme of Christian growth and development. Charlemont in particular is not as perfect a character in the play's opening scenes as he is by the conclusion. At least part of his virtue must be learned, and the process of learning the lessons of the play engages him in at least some active movement.

Charlemont's learning takes the form of several errors or false starts, the falseness of which is quickly made apparent to him. Thus, he attempts to go into battle against the wishes of his father, which forces him to try to convince his father he is right, to accept D'amvile's aid, financial and "moral." This ultimately results in Montferrer's death and Charlemont's imprisonment. Later, when Charlemont is visited by his father's ghost, he does not at first believe that the ghost is real:

> O my affrighted soule! what feareful dreame
> Was this that wak'd mee? Dreames are but the rais'd
> Impressions of premeditated things,
> By serious apprehension left upon
> Our mindes, or else th' imaginary shapes
> Of objects proper to th' complexion, or
> The dispositions of our bodyes.
>
> (II. vi. 29–35)

Paralleling D'amville's discussion of the thunder and lightning only a few lines earlier, Charlemont is attempting to explain away a supernatural manifestation as a natural phenomena. Unlike D'amville, Charlemont soon learns he is mistaken. The ghost appears a second time, and Charlemont exclaims: "O pardon me! my doubtfull heart was slow/ To credit that which I did feare to know" (II. vi. 78–79). Here we see Charlemont learning one of the most important lessons of the play—contrasted with D'amville's failure to learn the same lesson in very similar circumstances. In full view of the audience, Charlemont discovers that the divine is actively engaged in this world. The "natural" explanation of supernatural phenomena is a dangerous misapprehension. What the ghost says, of course, is directly related to what is proven by its existence—that the King of kings is working toward the "sucesse of things" and that Charlemont must learn to acquiesce patiently in that solution.

Again, when Charlemont has returned to find his father dead and
his lover stolen, he reacts "naturally" by striking out—in this case,
at Sebastian, the son of D'amville. He behaves, in other words, like
a revenger and not like a Christian:

> CHARLEMONT: Th'art a villaine; and the Sonne of a villaine.
> SEBASTIAN: You lye. *Fight*
> SEBASTIAN *is downe.*
> CHARLEMONT: Have at thee.
> *Enter the Ghost of* MONTERRERS.
> Revenge to thee Ile dedicate this worke.
>
> (III. ii. 39–44)

But, of course, in *The Atheist's Tragedy* this sort of "worke" is not
the province of man, and acts dedicated to revenge are a sacrilege.
The ghost, a polar opposite of the traditional ghost of the revenge
tragedy, far from goading his son into revenge, counsels him away
from it:

> MONTFERRERS: Hold Charlemont!
> Let him revenge my murder, and thy wrongs,
> To whom the Justice of Revenger belongs.
>   *Exit.*
> CHARLEMONT: You torture me betweene the passion of
> My bloud, and the religion of my soule.
>   SEBASTIAN *rises.*
> SEBASTIAN: A good honest fellow.
>
> (III. ii. 45–52)

It is just the torture between the passion of the blood and the
religion of the soul that can make a revenge play—be it *Hamlet, The
Spanish Tragedy,* or even *The Revenger's Tragedy*—into a tragedy.
The "natural" passion to right the wrongs done to one and the
Christian message of patience and divine vengeance can act as ir-
reconcilable forces, destroying a tragic hero caught between them.
But, in *The Atheist's Tragedy* Charlemont never comes closer to
achieving tragic stature than in his fight with Sebastian: it is not very
close. Rather than being caught between the revenge ethic and
Christian morality, Charlemont moves from the former to the latter.
In other words, Tourneur creates a hero who denies that the overwhelming ethical dilemma of *Hamlet* is a problem at all. Rather,

through the constant intervention of the supernatural, Charlemont comes to understand that the world is governed by a strong and ever-present moral force, which will actively work to oppose evil.

Charlemont learns this lesson so well that by the beginning of Act 5 he is actually eager to abandon this world and move on to the next:

> *D'amville!* to shew thee with what light respect,
> I value Death and thy insulting pride;
> Thus like a warlike Navie on the Sea,
> Bound for the conquest of some wealthie land,
> Pass'd through the stormie troubles of this life,
> And now arriv'd upon the armed coast;
> In expectation of the victorie,
> Whose honour lies beyond this exigent;
> Through mortall danger with an active spirit
> Thus I aspire to undergoe my death. *Leaps up the Scaffold.*
> (V. ii. 135–44)

Charlemont and Castabella stand as a clear contrast to D'amville and Levidulcia as the work's collective hero. In a play which affirms as an important theme the ethical virtue derived from a denial of worldly action, Tourneur faces the problem of an absence of dramatic action on the part of his protagonists. His solution lies in the heroic battle with (and conquest of) evil through learning and defending virtue.

There remains one character of some importance, Sebastian, whose role in *The Atheist's Tragedy* should be explicated. Although Sebastian is less of a major figure in the play than either the two atheists or the two Christians, he is perhaps more interesting than either pair. While D'amville, Levidulcia, Charlemont, and Castabella offer interesting intellectual and ethical configurations and contrasts, they remain largely intellectual creations. As personfications of virtues and vices they may at times move toward complexity in their delineations and interrelations, but they nevertheless must remain uncomplicated and one dimensional figures. Not so Sebastian. Although there is clearly a unity to his actions, Sebastian's nature and motives seem ambiguous, cloudy, ever shifting. He is perhaps the only really human character in the play.

Sebastian cheats and schemes with no more ethical regret than D'amville, as in his underhanded affair with Levidulcia. He is unaffected by the fact that he is committing adultery. On the other hand,

he is capable of reacting to the deviousness of others with a brave
and clear honesty, as witness his cry of "rape!" at the marriage of
Roussard and Castabella. He has no qualms about accepting money
from D'amville (whom he knows to be a villain) for fighting with
Charlemont (whom he knows to be honest)— and no qualms about
turning around and using the same money to free Charlemont.

This complex humanity, however, does not exclude Sebastian
from the clear allegorical scheme of the drama. Indeed, Sebastian
may be seen as in many ways the keystone of the morality play
structure of Tourneur's work. His very complexity, obscure motivation, and contradictory actions render him a clear type of the
"natural man." Sebastian, unlike D'amville, is not a worshipper of
nature—he is simply its creation. Unlike D'amville, Sebastian has
no quarrel with the universal moral order, but unlike Charlemont
and Castabella, he has no understanding of it. While he is a person
of basically decent impulses, he remains tied to the impulsive. He is
without the means of separating a noble urge from a base one.
Sebastian, as Levin observes, acts on the basis of "emotional impulse, a spontaneous, almost physical reflex," and as such, he il-
luminates the "distinction between true virtue . . . and mere good
nature."[11]

The possible configurations of this intriguing cast of characters
seem to beg for schematic representation. One can, with Murray,
divide the play into three categories of character: the sensualists,
the rationalists, and the Christians, and produce a pattern of this
sort:[12]

Christians	Atheists
Charlemont, Castabella	Rationalists: D'amville
	Sensualists: Levidulcia and
	minor characters.

Levin arranges the play's major characters in a rectangular
framework, with one axis for good and evil, another for rationalism
and sensualism:[13]

Good	Evil
Rational: Charlemont	
Castabella	D'amville
Sensual: Sebastian	Levidulcia

Finally, the characters can be arranged simply in terms of their qualities and fates. In such a pattern, Sebastian falls squarely in the middle, since, like most men, he combines the angelic and the animal:

Atheists	*Honest Men*
D'amville: rational	Charlemont: patient
Sebastian: natural man	
Levidulcia: sensual	Castabella: chaste

No matter how these characters are arranged, however, a pattern is clear. All the major characters of *The Atheist's Tragedy* represent ethical qualities which are defined intrinsically through the character's own actions and words,and extrinsically through contrasts and similarities to the words and actions of all the other major characters of the play. The pattern, when seen as a totality, presents a moral vision of man and his world. Sebastian is important in such a pattern, for he is the final prooof of its rather chilling rigor: for all his attractiveness, his basically good nature, and his decent impulses and actions, Sebastian falls ignominiously. He is murdered in squalid surroundings for sordid reasons. The ever-watchful God who will work miracles for Charlemont and Castabella will not intervene in the case of Sebastian. Tourneur's Christianity may be simple—even, to some, simpleminded—but its severity can be measured by its sting.

III *Theme*

Since *The Atheist's Tragedy* is an overtly moral play, and its morality is overtly traditional, it is easy to see the drama as a far simpler artifact than it actually is: Madelaine Doran, not an unsophisticated critic, observes that "Tourneur . . . keeps the fable moving so closely to an unexamined ethical formula that its full possibilities are never examined."[14] Doran is not the only critic of the Renaissance drama who takes such a view of this work. For. T. S. Eliot, the play "adds nothing at all to what the other play has given us. . . ." Indeed, for Eliot, all that was offered by *The Atheist's Tragedy* over *The Revenger's Tragedy* was "more regular verse, more conventional scenes."[15]

To those who find the play simpleminded, its theme seems incredibly childish. Doran states this most baldly: "*The Atheist's*

Tragedy appears to mean that to be an atheist is, on the whole, a bad thing. But what does *King Lear* mean?"[16] One is tempted to respond that if this play "means" only that to be an atheist is a bad thing, then perhaps *King Lear* means that old men can be troublesome!

The idea here seems to be that since Tourneur presents a traditionalistic moral viewpoint, the morality of the play is, by definition, unexamined. This is a flabby and itself unexamined notion. It seems the equivalent of saying that since St. Augustine died a good Christian, he never thought about God. Tourneur does carefully examine moral questions before he arrives at his conclusions. Far from a stale rehashing of inherited moral attitudes, the play emerges as a bold and original statement of traditional beliefs.

Clearly *The Atheist's Tragedy* comes out of the literary tradition of the Kydian revenger tragedy discussed earlier: its hero has been done a great injustice—through both a murder in the family and an attack on his beloved—by a villain beyond the reach of the social law. There is a ghost; a final scene in which the villain is done in and the revenge accomplished; ominous portents, graveyards, dark nights, murderous accomplices, etc. All the trappings of the conventional revenge play are here. But, equally clearly, Tourneur does not accept the basic moral premises of the entire revenge tradition. Occasionally critics have seen the play as simply a "painful compromise" between the Kydian tradition and religious morality. Actually, that compromise occurs in the greater revenge plays of the period, in which the "tension between the contrary demands of divine law and retribution as a debt of honor" is resolved in tragedy.[17] *The Atheist's Tragedy* is a lesser but unique play in that it removes itself from the convention which inspired it by virtually cannonizing the nonrevenging revenger.

This unconventional use of the revenge motif moves Tourneur's play far beyond the "atheism is bad" level. It broadens the definition of "atheism" as to make its condemnation not a truism but a profound act of faith.

The Atheist's Tragedy, for all its flaws, is a play which seeks and finds a comprehensive philosophy of man and his world. It represents, says Jenkins, "a searching inquiry into the foundations of human life, a desire to understand its purpose and to formulate a view of man's position in the universe."[18] Tourneur sees the natural universe, including much of "human nature," as unredeemably vicious. Nature is a "ravening and dominating force, destroying and urging on the destroyer."[19] This nature manifests itself in human beings as an absolute prediliction to sin and depravity. Such a view of nature and human nature is derived as much from characters like Sebastian who are not monsters, as it is from the conscious naturalists like Levidulcia and D'amville. It is easy to condemn the latter, very hard the former.

The satiric elements of *The Atheist's Tragedy* even demolish those institutional aspects of human life and society which medieval and Renaissance optimists might see as capable of moving such a corrupted world toward salvation. The church, the state, the court, the family do not save men from themselves but simply encourage, accelerate, and magnify their fall: "The nearer the Church; the further from God" (I. iv. 150–51).

D'amville, the atheist, materialist, rationalist, naturalist, is the greatest victim of this evil natural universe. He puts all his hope and faith in "nature"—the superficialities of the material world—and thus offers himself up as the willing victim of fortune. This is the overwhelming irony of the play, from which all the lesser ironies spring: the naturalists deliberately throw themselves into the hands of a ravening power which can only destroy them, because it is a power tuned solely to destruction. The believers in human reason are the least rational of men.

From within this framework emerges the central thematic question of *The Atheist's Tragedy:* how may a good man live in a world corrupted by the reality of sin and death? The answer lies in the recognition of a power beyond nature which, if accepted with humility and faith, can guide a person through the thicket of an evil world to salvation.

It is through his eagerness to establish a God who is distinctly over and above nature that Tourneur creates those moments of coincidence and improbable action which have disturbed so many readers of *The Atheist's Tragedy.* The probable, after all, is the mechanism of the material universe. It is the improbable, the interruption of the expected and ordinary course of events, which shows clearly the hand of God. In the natural world we do not expect a display of thunder and lightning to follow a declaration of atheism. But, in a sense, if thunder and lightning *could not* be made to order in response to such a statement, then the statement would be true.

The honest men, like Charlemont and Castabella, must recognize both these worlds, the natural and the supernatural. Their life in the first must be guided solely by their consideration of the second. To Tourneur—and many Jacobeans including James I himself—such a recognition manifests itself in a philosophy of life which today may appear shockingly reactionary. The honest man understands his place in the world, and he understands that the world is evil. At its most extreme, Tourneur's philosophy might condemn social work as atheism. The person who attempts to change society—even for the better—is simply immersing himself in the muck of an evil world, and when a man goes to bed with a skunk, the skunk does not wake up smelling like a man. The good man is the submissive man. He submits to the order of things, knowing that that order is ultimately divine. He does not acquiesce in evil works, but he does not confuse himself with God and judge or punish them. If threatened with death, like Charlemont, he accepts the possibility with joy—death is the only way out of a polluted and polluting world. On the other hand, he becomes neither a suicide nor a hermit, for both attempt to deny, and thus, subvert, the God-given order. Patience is the honest man's revenge—not only for crimes done to him, but for a criminal world.

IV   Other Elements

Once one recognizes the basic ethical structure of *The Atheist's Tragedy*, achieved through the allegorical movements of plot and character, it is fascinating to note the careful and complete manner in which other elements of the dramatist's craft have been pressed into the service of the play's central theme. In terms of literary techniques and influences, Tourneur's drama is eclectic, but its eclecticism is entirely at the service of its main movement.

Like *The Revenger's Tragedy*, *The Atheist's Tragedy* is frequently satiric. Unlike the former, the latter play never gives the impression of developing satire for its own sake. We have already noted that the prime function of the work's satire is to illuminate more fully the degree of corruption of human and worldly nature, particularly as manifested in man's social institutions. The church, and the precisionist, middle-class Puritan denominations in particular, come under heavy fire. The most ludicrous satiric target of the play is "Languebeau Snuffe, a Puritaine." Snuffe is a familiar enough figure from the satire of the times, the impure Puritan, the hypocrite cleric. While quick enough to condemn the sins of the flesh in others, he is himself the eager victim of the same sins:

I perceive the puritie of my conversation is us'd but for a propertie to cover the uncleanenesse of their purposes. The very contemplation o' the thing, makes the spirit of the flesh begin to wriggle in my bloud. . . . Temptation has prevail'd over mee; and I will attempt to make it overcome her. (IV. i. 73–80)

The portrait of this Jacobean Tartuffe is rendered more ridiculous by Snuffe's ignorance and stupidity—which frequently serve to reveal his true nature when he is at his most hypocritical. Thus his first line of the play, greeting the chaste Charlemont and Castabella, "I salute you both with the spirit of copulation . . ." (I. ii. 109).

We are never allowed, however, to revel in this comical denunciation of a false Puritan without being reminded of his larger purpose within the allegory of *The Atheist's Tragedy*. His very name suggests that purpose: to "snuffe" is to extinguish or put out a light. Languebeau is by profession a candlemaker who has attempted to snuff out his real identity through an assumed role. But more importantly, he is a clergyman who has done all within his power to extinguish and darken the light of God. When Sebastian remarks that the nearer the church, the further from God, he is simply putting into words what Snuffe has already demonstrated in action. The church in the world—because it is influenced by men and because men are Snuffes—is a false road to enlightenment. Tourneur, in his own unique fashion, has turned a satiric pun on the name of a minor character into a telling moral statement.

The Atheist's Tragedy is as ironic as it is satiric, and again, the comparison with *The Revenger's Tragedy* is illuminating. In the latter the principal burden carried by irony is one of demonstrating precisely how evil tends to destroy itself—amoral Machiavellian schemes all seem to contain within themselves the mechanism for destroying the schemer. In *The Atheist's Tragedy*, a new dimension is added. Here evil remains destructive, but the agency of this destruction is far more overtly external, supernatural. Thus, the irony of the play derives from the knowledge of the audience that justice belongs to the King of kings, and that it cannot be averted. This knowledge is constantly reinforced by the play's ghosts and supernatural occurrences, the most dramatic and ironic of which is of course D'amville's surprising self-murder at the conclusion. Irony arises when the drama's evil characters proclaim their disbelief in phenomena whose existence the audience clearly sees, and proudly proclaim that those who believe in such things are fools—thus demonstrating conclusively their own foolishness. Again, the literary technique is integrated completely into the overall aims and structure of the play.

The same can—and has—been said concerning the drama's poetic style. Almost every student of Tourneur's works has noted the rather pronounced differences between the styles of Tourneur's two tragedies. To many, these differences constitute a weakening of poetic powers: "In the verse of *The Atheist's Tragedy* concentration has given way to discursiveness, metaphor to simile, intensity to slackness."[20] T. S. Eliot damns Tourneur's poetry with very faint praise: ". . . there is no development, no fresh inspiration; only the skillful but uninspired use of a greater metrical variety [than that of *The Revenger's Tragedy*]."[21]

Surprisingly, those who seem unimpressed with the verse of the play seem to agree with those of a more positive persuasion as to the characteristics of that verse. It is a far slower, more careful, rationally constructed style than that of *The Revenger's Tragedy*. Critics themselves are drawn to metaphor to describe the lightninglike style of *The Revenger's Tragedy* with its almost metaphysical flashes of poetic insight. Here, however, the poet appears at best a careful and conscious craftsman: it is appropriate that one of the major groups of images in the latter play is of building. In the second work, the speeches tend to be "expository" and have a "strictly logical structure."[22] For example, here is an argument for female sexuality in *The Atheist's Tragedy:*

> Preferr'st th' affection of an absent Love,
> Before the sweet possession of a·man;
> The barren minde before the fruitful body;
> Where our creation has no reference
> To man; but in his body: being made
> Onely for generation; which (unlesse
> Our children can be gotten by conceit)
> Must from the body come.
>
> (I. iv. 83–90)

In *The Revenger's Tragedy:*

> But theres a cold curse layd upon all Maydes,
> Whilst others clip the Sunne they clasp the shades!
> Virginity is paradice, lockt up.
>
> (II. i. 174–76)

While the verse of *The Atheist's Tragedy* clearly lacks the fire of that of *The Revenger's Tragedy*, it exhibits a greater sense of decorum. There is a precise "fitting of language to character" and to theme.[23] Each speech, with its logical structure from premise to conclusion, fits into a strictly logical plot, which moves similarly through an examination of various premises to their respective conclusions. Ekeblad observes that "The whole play follows the pattern of a gradually progressing argument: scenes and incidents are arranged so as to show, first the postulates on which Evil bases its works and the wrongness of which must be apparent . . . from the very first lines, then its actual workings, and finally its debacle."[24] Lightning is an appropriate way to illuminate a dark world; logic and craftsmanship an equally appropriate way to explain it.

Nowhere is the craftsmanship of Tourneur's later style more apparent than in the play's imagery. Three major image groups amply illustrate this craft: images of building, water, and light.

The building imagery of *The Atheist's Tragedy* is most particularized and precise. It is "drawn exclusively from one aspect, the founding, raising, and subsequent fall of a building . . . . [used] to illustrate the founding, rearing, and overthrowing of the family of D'amville."[25] D'amville points to the spot where Montferrers has just been killed, and the rock which crushed his skull, and exults (in a rather obvious parody of the New Testament): "Upon this ground Ile build my Manour-house; / And this shall be the chiefest corner stone" (II. iv. 118–19). At the conclusion of the play, D'amville watches his son die, and laments:

> His gasping sighs are like the falling noise
> Of some great building when the ground-worke breakes.
> On these two pillars stood the stately frame,
> And architecture of my loftie house.
> An Earthquake shakes 'em. The foundation shrinkes.
>
> (V. i. 92–96)

Between these two points, the building imagery carefully follows the course of the House of D'amville.

This image sequence may not be described as inspired—it clearly lacks the quality of surprise which, with appropriateness, characterized the best imagery of *The Revenger's Tragedy*. But if these building images are a bit pedestrian, they are at the same time almost perfectly workmanlike tools to communicate the notions of

grand rise and ruinous fall. Tourneur is trying to show the fruitless-
ness of striving to build glory on this earth, and the noble house
built on a shaky foundation of disbelief, murder, and sin, conveys
this idea precisely.

The thematic contrasts between the atheists and the honest men
are also amply illustrated through images of water and light. In both
cases, the same imagery is used with widely different meanings for
the different sets of characters.

The "liquid" imagery of *The Atheist's Tragedy* ("blood in the
human veins and arteries or, at the level of the macrocosm, of water
in springs and rivers")[26] sharply differentiates between atheists and
believers. To the atheists, blood, like water, is a natural force, rush-
ing faster and faster to its goal. It is a "destroying river of lust":[27] "a
modest innocence/ Of bloud; whose unmoov'd streame was never
drawne/ Into the current of affection" (I. iv. 6–8); "The wanton
streame, like a strumpet . . ."(IV. i. 37); "Those wanton running
waters" (IV. i. 43); "the Spring of lust which you preserv'd; And
nourish'd; ranne the effusion of that bloud" (V. ii. 31–32). Contrasted to this gushing lust is the pure water of the honest men.[28]
Castabella repeatedly refers to her tears, the

> jewels of my love
> Dissolved into grief: and fall upon
> His blasted Spring; as Aprill dewe, upon
> A sweet young blossome. . . .
>
> (III. i. 68–71)

As Charlemont prepares to die, he sees himself "like a warlike Navie
on the Sea/Bound for the conquest of some wealthie land . . ." (V. ii.
137–38).

In the final scene, before D'amville attempts to execute Charlemont and Castabella, he describes his condition and prescribes himself an (ineffective) cure in terms of liquids:

> This argument of death congeals my bloud.
> Colde feare with apprehension of thy end,
> Hath frozen up the rivers of my veins.—*A glasse of wine.*
> I must drinke wine to warm mee, and dissolve
> The obstruction. . . .
>
> (V. ii. 217–21)

Charlemont, on the other hand, wants only water:

CHARLEMONT: Is this water?
SERVANT: Water Sir.—a glasse of water.
CHARLEMONT: Come thou cleare embleme of coole temperance.
(V. ii. 228–30)

The final comparison could not be made clearer. The wine of D'am-ville is a kind of antisacramental rite, a final attempt to set into motion the destructive rivers of blood which have characterized the atheists. It fails. The clear emblem of cool temperance, Charle-mont's glass of water, invokes Castabella's tears, the renewing and rejuvenating gift of the heavens.

Similarly, the use of light and light imagery in the play helps to define the differences between the atheists and the honest men. As Murray points out, this takes the form of a "conflict of true and false lights."[29] Reason is a false light to guide man, upon which D'amville bases his career. The murder of Montferrers is dependent upon extinguishing the lights carried by the servants accompanying the old baron and his evil brother; D'amville praises "black night; Thou beauteous Mistresse of a murder" (II. iv. 203–4). Contrasting these false lights of evil are the true lights of divinity, particularly the stars. In an essay on "Tourneur and the Stars," Tompkins asserts that, "During the first three acts the stars, which are symbols and instruments of the divine government of the world, are hidden!":[30] The point is amply incorporated in the text: "Musicke. A banquet. In the night" (s.d. II. i. 1–2); "The skie is darke . . ." (II. ii. 61); "T'is exceeding darke" (II. iv. 14); "Eternal darkenesse damne you . . ." (II. iv. 28); "Then darkenesse did/ Protect the execution of the worke" (II. iv. 150–51). By Act 4 the night is becoming clearer; D'amville in the churchyard mistakes a "faire white cloude" (IV. iii. 263) for a ghost. The stars whose influence D'amville has consistently mocked turn against him. At one of the ironic high points of the play, D'amville prepares to press charges of murder against Charlemont:

Nature thou are a Traytor to my soule.
Thou hast abus'd my trust. I will complaine
To a superiour Court, to right my wrong.
I'le prove thee a forger of false assurances
In yound' Starre chamber thou shalt answere it.
(V. i. 140–44)

The irony arises because D'amville is far more accurate than he knows. The superior court, the true star chamber, does indeed give him justice, and in so doing proves which is the supreme and only true light. The contrast between atheists and honest men is illuminated through the imagistic gulf between the stars and Snuffe!

V Literary Antecedents

The Atheist's Tragedy, while clearly a unique drama, is nevertheless influenced by diverse literary sources. The study of such influences and the intricate interrelationships between Renaissance plays is a fascinating field, but of only limited intrinsic importance in the consideration of any given work of art. We need not, therefore, devote too much time to discussion of, for instance, the complexities of the thematic relations between The Atheist's Tragedy and Chapman's Bussy plays, but it is worth noting that such relations exist.

Chapman's two plays—Bussy d'Ambois (ca. 1603) and The Revenge of Bussy d'Ambois (ca. 1610)—clearly contribute much to The Atheist's Tragedy. Most obviously, they contribute the names of Tourneur's main characters. Chapman's d'Ambois becomes D'amville, his Clermont is Tourneur's Charlemont. Chapman's works deal with a powerful individualist (Bussy), murder, revenge, stoicism, rationalism, all important elements in The Atheist's Tragedy. Tourneur's play, however, represents a "christianization" of Chapman's materials. Where Chapman's ideal seems to be a stoical rationalism, Tourneur splits these characteristics, producing a rationalistic villain, and a Christian-stoic hero. According to C. Leech,

Tourneur had before him the supreme individualist in Bussy, in Clermont the man suspicious of action. These two figures undergo transformation in D'amville and Charlemont. [Tourneur's transformations of Chapman's materials, then, may be seen as a] retort to Chapman's Bussy plays; he takes a hint from Clermont's reluctance to avenge his brother, he echoes the names of d'Ambois and Clermont, but his sentence of damnation is ready for the man without a curb on his will and he gives to Charlemont reasons for inaction which never occurred to Clermont d'Ambois.[31]

If Tourneur was perhaps moved to compose The Atheist's Tragedy partially in response to Chapman's work, in the actual writing of his play he is nevertheless more deeply influenced by other dramatists. Tourneur seems to have been a particularly careful reader of Shakespeare—an inclination which may well be taken as a compliment to his literary and theatrical taste. There are numerous verbal echoes of Shakespeare's works, particularly *King Lear*, in the play. D'amville's attitudes toward nature surely owe some debt to Edmund, Shakespeare's exponent of a similar naturalistic philosophy. Similarly, *The Atheist's Tragedy*'s discussion of the stars bears comparison with the same subject in *King Lear*. Hamlet, of course, raised most seriously the questions of revenge and morality with which Tourneur deals, and it seems unlikely that *The Atheist's Tragedy* could have been written had there been no *Hamlet* to lead the way. Irving Ribner sees a relationship between the "sense of affirmation" in Tourneur's play and in "Shakespeare's tragedy of apostasy, *Macbeth*."[32] We have already noted the possible influence of Jonson's *Volpone* and Marlowe's *The Jew of Malta* upon D'amville's materialism. Moreover, it was Marlowe who introduced into the English theater the figure of the dominating, tragically isolated hero-villain, the questioner of the universe, challenger of God and man. If it is difficult to imagine *The Atheist's Tragedy* being written outside of a tradition which included *Hamlet*, it is almost impossible to believe that Tourneur could have conceived the central atheist of his play without the germinal example of Marlowe's "over-reachers."

As the brief summary above should make clear, Tourneur's second known play was hardly created in a literary vacuum. Tourneur was probably moved, at least in part, to create his tragedy of the atheist by one of the minor dramatists of his time, and in the writing of his work was heavily influenced by the major figures of the Elizabethan stage. Nevertheless, the product of this study and carefully conventionalized craftsmanship remains one of the most distinctive of all the works written for that stage. The strength and intensity of its ethical theme serve to unify it and render it anything but an anthology of other men's work. *The Atheist's Tragedy* is not one of the best plays ever written, but it is one of the most intriguingly honest plays of its, or any, time.

CHAPTER 6

Late Minor Works

TOURNEUR'S three late works are undeniably minor. They do, however, merit brief study, each work in itself, in comparison with each other, and within the context of Tourneur's more significant efforts. All three are elegies. *A Funerall Poeme Upon the death of Sir Francis Vere* was entered in the Stationers' Register in October, 1609, its subject having died at the end of August. *The Character of Robert, Earl of Salisbury* was almost certainly written shortly after Salisbury's death in 1612. And on Christmas day of the same year appeared Tourneur's *A Griefe on the Death of Prince Henrie* mourning the prince who died on November 6.

All three works commemorate the death of an important public figure: Vere was a famous soldier; Salisbury, the leading politician of his time: and Henry, of course, the Prince of Wales. Of these three notable subjects, Tourneur had some personal acquaintance with Vere, having served under him as a soldier in the Netherlands. Tourneur also served the Cecils—at least after 1612, but it is highly unlikely that he knew Robert, earl of Salisbury as anything other than a respected public man and, perhaps, a distant family retainer. It is of course clear that Tourneur had no personal acquaintanceship with Prince Henry, the eldest son of King James I. Further relationships and differences between these three works will become apparent after closer examination of each.

I *Vere*

A Funeral Poem (the full title is "A Funerall Poeme Upon the Death of the Most Worthie and True Soldier, Sir Francis Vere") is the longest of these three works. It consists of 604 lines of rhyming couplets (lacking, of course, the strong end-stopping characteristic of the eighteenth-century heroic couplet); for example,

Thy Earth's return'd to Earth, from whence it came;
But from thy Spirit rize thy worthy Fame,
Immortall Vere; and that shall never dye;
But with it live to all posteritie.

(1–4)

An elegy, of course, does not have a plot—it is, by formal necessity, a complimentary description of the deceased. But the elegiac
form does invite an artistically ordered pattern of biographical reve-
lations which may be said to take the place of a plot. *A Funeral Poem*
is no exception. The poem is framed by an introduction and conclusion which assert Vere's general claim to eternal fame. The interven-
ing larger portion of the work consists of a catalog of those virtues of
the deceased which Tourneur feels justify this claim. These are, in
order, a disciplined mind; a devotion to public service; a capacity for
stern, patient, and self-sacrificing leadership; and an heroic combination of fighting spirit and crafty intelligence.

Keeping this summary of the "plot" or pattern of the work in
mind, it is interesting and worthwhile to examine the major aspects
of the poem in greater detail, with an eye toward the poetic
strategies which governed Tourneur's decisions of both inclusion
and exclusion in his elegy. It is intriguing to note, for example, the
personality characteristics in which Tourneur is interested—the
movement of *A Funeral Poem* is, in a limited way, a chart of Tourneur's own ethical situation. In this manner, the poem may tell us
more about Tourneur's morality than about Vere's.

The elegy begins and ends with a conventional assertion that the
fame of its subject will be eternal (see lines 1–4 quoted above).
Tourneur expresses this concept in a metaphor reminiscent of *The
Transformed Metamorphosis*, *The Revenger's Tragedy* and *The
Atheist's Tragedy*:

How can the Memory of such a Spirit,
Whose Actions ev'n of Envie got his Merit
Acknowledgement, Subscription, approbation;
And made it clearly shine through Emulation,
Which with Contracted Cloudes did interpose,
Between the world and him, to darken those
Illustrious honours of his noble worth

Which his esentiall Souldiership brought forth;
Be ever ruin'd.

(5–13)

Vere, like all of Tourneur's heroes, lives in a "dark" world. Like
Mavortio of *The Transformed Metamorphosis*, Vere is a light
fighting against this darkness, or at least, shining through it. Unlike
Mavortio, Vere is a real person.

Tourneur then turns to the specific qualities of Vere he wishes to
praise. He begins with "his minde . . . like an empire, rich and
strong" (36). This powerful mind was both a gift of nature and the
result of careful development. Its loftiest quality was its moderation . . . "so sweet and temperate a seate/ Without th' extremities of
cold or heate" (53–54). Strength and moderation of mind gave to
Vere, Tourneur suggests, a "discipline" admirably suited to the
military life: "He was a Souldier bourne, as well as bred" (92). He
knew how both to command and to obey.

While Vere is described as one who "gave himselfe unto the
publique cause" (135), he never courted public favor nor became
obsequious. Public service was his aim; not popularity.

Tourneur praises Vere's qualities as a leader. He personally took
time to reward the deserving, thus earning the loyalty and gratitude
of his men. Moreover, he himself provided the example of merit and
honor for his men to follow—he was always "i' th' front/ Of danger"
(172–73), and "his Action still was wont/ To lead the way to honour"
(171–72). As a leader, Vere recognized the need for stern discipline.
Tourneur says that Vere could be strict, recognizing that by making
an example of one offender among the soldiers, he could prevent
many others from straying. Nevertheless, Tourneur says, his reputation for cruelty was not deserved. Actually strong punishment was
a kindness, since it

did as happily prevent
The just necessitie of punishment
Of many lives which under a milder course
Presumption would incurre.

(255–58)

Moreover, Vere was never harsh in private matters. In this, and all
other things, he never let passion rule him: "He had a mind so

temperatelie cleare/ And free from passion . . ." (304–5). The absence of passion enabled Vere to be patient when patience was called for. Patience here, as in *The Atheist's Tragedy,* is considered almost an active quality—"the strength of patience" (310). Discipline and patience made Vere a man always valued in council, since he combined truth with mildness.

Vere's military writings, says Tourneur, demonstrate his quick and full "understanding"—an ability to quickly grasp a situation and plan a course of action designed to respond to it. As a consequence, when, in the field, prompt action was necessary, Vere was always prepared for it.

These qualities of mind do not negate the fact that Tourneur's elegiac protagonist had a strong fighting spirit: he combined "fortitude" and "wisedome." Yet, while he was never fearful, he was also never rash, but always an advocate and an example of balanced action. Tourneur spends some time moralizing upon the necessity of this balancing between cowardice and foolhardy courage—as does Shakespeare in the *Henry IV* plays. He also points out that such a balance characterized Vere from the beginnings of his career, and thus characterized him as a man, not simply as a general.

As a military strategist, Vere was not above craft:

> And what his sword could not directly hit;
> He circumvented by the power of wit.
> Using that licence (onely) which in warre
> Hath just allowance. . . .
>
> (551–54)

Like Machiavelli's ideal prince, the general could combine the strength of a lion with the cunning of the fox.

Finally, Tourneur asserts, Vere's record of success is all that is needed to prove he possessed all these qualities, particularly the victorious battles of "Nieuport and Ostend/ (Those famous services)" (575–76). Even in a time of peace the nobility Vere demonstrated guaranteed that his "Monument, while Historie doth last;/ Shall never be forgotten or derac'd" (603–4).

The few critics who have commented upon *A Funeral Poem* find in it two facets of some importance—historical and stylistic. Historically, the poem helps to define Tourneur's life and is a major piece of evidence concerning his early years as a soldier.[1] The literary importance of the work is generally found in "its unadorned and straightforward manner, which is appropriate to the manly honest character of its subject."[2] This style, says Nicoll, lacks "the majestic sweep of inspired poetry," but does possess "at least a convenient and competent medium for the expression of an admiration, obviously sincere. . . ."[3]

Perhaps the most important aspect of *A Funeral Poem*, however, appears when it is placed within a chronological perspective. This work was written in 1609; *The Revenger's Tragedy* was entered in The Stationers' Register in 1607; and *The Atheist's Tragedy* was first published in 1611. This poem, then, occupies a central position in the chronology of Tourneur's works: on the near sides, as it were, are the two major dramas. In the distant past, *The Transformed Metamorphosis* and *Laugh and Lie Down;* in the distant future, *The Character of Salisbury* and *A Grief for Prince Henry.*

We have already noted one theme which dominates Tourneur's plays and poems, a theme always repeated but never duplicated, developing from work to work. This is the theme of the good individual in an evil world. In *The Transformed Metamorphosis,* Tourneur has to resort to mythologizing his Christ-like saviour hero Mavortio, a device which succeeds in stating the problem but fails to move toward a credible solution. In *The Revenger's Tragedy,* Vindice demonstrates how an essentially good man becomes evil by attempting to deal with an evil world in worldly terms. Charlemont and Castabella, in *The Atheist's Tragedy,* prove that it is possible to remain good when surrounded by evil through an avoidance of the worldly, a reliance upon divine providence, the suppression of passion, and the cultivation of patience. *A Funeral Poem* is a short and incomplete portrait of a real man whom Tourneur seems to thinks really lived his life in the pattern of the honest men of *The Atheist's Tragedy.* In *A Funeral Poem,* Vere is "so portrayed as to resemble the ideal Stoic hero. Vere was, says Tourneur, sweet and temperate, self-sufficient, free from passion, moved by neither fear nor anger."[4] He is, like both Tourneur himself and Charlemont, a soldier and a civil servant. Like Tourneur and Charlemont, Vere does not believe in private revenge:

> Offences done against his owne estate,
> (Which alwayes doth more strongly aggravate
> The weight of injurie to private sense,

> Then publique apprehension of offence;
> And stirres mens passions more;) have often times
> Subduced the Malefactors for those crimes,
> Into the hands of Justice: where he might
> With approbation and consent of right,
> Have satisfied that Nature to the full;
> As well in punishments that justly pull
> On Death as other grevious penalties.
> And yet his hurt that from those faults did rise,
> And nearely touch'd him, never did incense
> Or move his mind. . . .
>
> (273–87)

The calmness and balanced patience which characterize the subject of *A Funeral Poem* prefigure the Christian stoicism of the heroes of *The Atheist's Tragedy*. *A Funeral Poem* is important in that it shows Tourneur moving from the fascinating but unsatisfactory disposition of an honest man in a dishonest world in *The Revenger's Tragedy* into the solutions of *The Atheist's Tragedy*.

II *Cecil*

Tourneur's "Character" of Robert Cecil, earl of Salisbury is, like the funeral poem for Vere, written in a style appropriate to its subject. It consists of 141 lines of tight, swift, economical prose. The "Character" briefly describes the private man behind the civil servant, then moves to Cecil as a public figure. Particular characteristics cited include articulateness, integrity, a sense of position, and independence. It is extremely utilitarian in its characterization of an extremely utilitarian man.

Tourneur begins, as one must in this case, by noting Cecil's parentage—"He came of a parente that Counseled the State . . ." (1). He notes that Cecil was deformed in body—perhaps a sign he was fated to become a statesman, since his courage and intelligence might otherwise have impelled him to a more active occupation. Cecil, as counselor, had the virtue of always being able to make himself understood, no matter to whom he was speaking or writing. His words

> were delyvered with such a dexteritie of clearness, that they were both Sweete to a curious eare, and easie to a Common; beinge Neither of Rudness, not affection.
>
> (27–29)

Not only did Cecil make himself understood, he also made himself accessible, and could listen as well as speak or write. He was also reliable, and his promise was always kept.

Tourneur says that Cecil, like Vere, never failed to put the public interest ahead of the private. Like Vere he showed this trait by refusing to court popularity:

> He had the moste safe pollicie in him, that can bee in an eminent subject; for he did not affect popularitie; And therein he was as faithfull to the state as to his owne ends; for popular Love belonges onely to majestie.
>
> (72–75)

A true servant of royalty, Cecil never failed to take the blame for severity, and to give others credit for his own generosity. This "grew to be a Cause of . . . Mallice to Him" (82–83). But nevertheless, the country never forgot his competence, and in a crisis always turned to him, saying, " 'This man doth not erre' " (89–90). He experienced all the possible situations which might confront the statesman, save only "a Civill warre; wherein his Judgment was the more worthie, for he prevented it" (101–2).

Cecil, a true Tourneur hero, eschewed revenge: "He never writte downe an Injurye done to him in redd ynke" (105–6). He did favors for many, but depended for favors for himself solely upon the king—which made him the surest of royal employees. That he was a religious man is proven by his will, in which "his relegeous faith is sett downe" (126). Those who inherit his job should be anxious to follow his example. They need fear no enemies, for "it hath not pleased God, to give anie of his detractors the witt to expresse themselves well against him" (139–41).

The subject of Tourneur's "Character" is one of the most fascinating personalities of the late Elizabethan and early Jacobean eras. We have discussed briefly Cecil's historical role during this period in Chapter 1. A few more personal details here will help to complete a brief portrait.

Cecil was the son of William Cecil, later Lord Burghley, chief counselor to Queen Elizabeth. William had risen to his position largely through foresight, energy, competence. His son Robert was a weak and sickly boy, whom his father trained rigorously and specifically to fill his position.

Somehow, to the modern sensibility, Lord Burghley's attempt to make his son in his own image would seem guaranteed to fail. It did not. Robert was, if anything, a better statesman than his father. From 1596 until 1598, father and son constituted the day to day government of England. From 1598, when William died, until 1601, Robert vied with Essex for the position closest to the queen. Essex won the glory—Robert won the battle. From 1601 until Elizabeth's death in 1603 Robert Cecil was England's first minister. During this period he carefully and delicately paved the way for the orderly succession of the crown upon the death of Elizabeth. Since James was the only logical candidate for the position, this might seem an easy job, but Elizabeth had always wanted to think herself immortal, and preparing for her death could easily be considered very close to treason. The succession did proceed calmly, and Robert Cecil was generally assumed—as Tourneur discretly asserts in the line quoted earlier—to have prevented civil war. Cecil was stuck with his greatest accomplishment, however: having delivered to James the crown, he was forced to watch, from the vantage point of James' first minister, his gift abused and misused. He tried to keep King James afloat, and almost succeeded. But like most other competent men in the service of James I, he was ultimately discredited—in 1611. He died a year later, and in the same year Tourneur wrote his "Character." That the "Character" never went beyond manuscript stage is, almost certainly, due to its honesty. Praise of one who had fallen from favor was not wise during the reigns of the Stuarts.

The Character of Salisbury is not only honest, but an insightful portrait which the judgment of history has upheld. Tourneur saw clearly Cecil's virtues—wide knowledge, an ability to make himself understood, a complete dedication to his position, and an utter pragmatism. Equally, Cecil's imperfections—of body and character—are not buried very far beneath the surface of the "Character": "craft" and "policy" are not in the vocabulary of the Elizabethan panegyrist. Tourneur does not hide the fact that Cecil's pragmatism and cunning brought him many enemies and much unpopularity. What Tourneur does present in *The Character of Salisbury* is a portrait of an almost perfect public servant. The "Character" does not convey much sense of a living, breathing, imperfect human being. Neither, perhaps, did its subject.

III *Prince Henry*

King James' eldest son, Henry, Prince of Wales, died early in November, 1612. A month and a half later, three elegies, by Cyril

Tourneur, John Webster, and Thomas Heywood, were entered in
the Stationers' Register. Since each elegy has a separate title page, it
appears likely that they were printed to be sold both together and
separately.[6] Tourneur's *A Grief on the Death of Prince Henry* is a
brief, formal, and at first reading relatively uninteresting work.

A Grief on the Death of Prince Henry begins with a dedication to
an unidentified "George Carie." It would be helpful to know who
this potential patron was, since his identity might cast some light
upon Tourneur's fairly sketchy biography. Given the present evidence, however, no identification is possible—there are too many
men whose names might be spelled "Carie" and no further way of
linking any of them to Tourneur.

In a brief address "To The Reader," Tourneur warns that the
subject of his poem is so mournful that the poem will be difficult to
read through the tears it inspires.

The poem proper begins with the statement that only the evil can
rejoice at the death of the young prince, "For now the President of
vertu's dead . . ." (11) Since the prince was such an emblem of
virtue, the poet asks what virtues can keep the rest of the world
alive, now that he has died. How, in fact, could he have died so
young, since even his pleasures were noble? Perhaps his death was
the beginning of some plague—at any rate,

> . . . twas to us a plague whereof Hee died.
> A plague but much more common to us, then
> The last great sicknesse.
>
> (42–44)

Old men mourn Prince Henry, since he was their children's
hope. The young will suffer even more, since they will have to live
on without him. But, the poet asks, is this argument valid? For, as
the case of the prince so sadly proved, the young can die before the
old.

But, Tourneur exclaims, the prince did not really die young at all:

> He liv'd a Man as long as any does.
> For (onelie) in those Minutes that wee give
> To Vertue, wee are Truelie said to live
> Men, and no longer
>
> (74–77)

The prince, then, was so virtuous that he lived a long life by comparison with lesser men.

A fictional and archetypical soldier is presented mourning the death of honor and nobility, lost with the prince: "Hee weepes. He weepes; that can more easilie/Weepe Bloud than Water" (94–95). The arts equally mourn his passing, but will continue to exist, if only to praise his memory.

The poem concludes by stating that the memory of the prince will continue as a model for all men, and that not only his memory, but his spirit and its virtuous influence, are immortal.

Following the 140-line poem proper, are two short verses, both signed "C. T." The first, "On the Representation of the Prince at His Funeralls" repeats the theme of the dual mourning of the military and peaceful arts: "souldiers griefe, and Scholars teares" (8). The second brief afterword is entitled "On the Succession." It is a rather strange piece, and since it is so short, it can be quoted here in full:

> The State of England hath beene oft opress'd
> By many great pretenders. Fewe posses'd
> The kingdomes title safelie, but when One
> Descended, and inherited alone.
> Prince Henrie saw his brother Charles was younger,
> There in Love (because Hee might live longer;)
> Gave way: and for the Kingdomes strengthening,
> He left but one Sonne to succeed the King.

The "Charles" of line 6 is, of course, the same Charles I whom Tourneur's countrymen beheaded about thirty years later. It is difficult to assess the implications of this brief poem. It would surely be naive to presume it means literally what it says—that Henry died on purpose to make the succession clearer. On the other hand, it seems overly suspicious to read into this little piece—which *was* published publicly—some sort of hint that, since Charles benefitted so greatly from Henry's death, he or his followers may have had a hand in it, or at least rejoiced in it: it is to be recalled that the poem asserts strongly that only the devil's disciples can be happy at the death of the young prince. Perhaps the poem only means to make it clear that the poet and his countrymen understood the political implications of the prince's death, and were a bit unhappy about those implications.

This explanation certainly fits within the historical context. It also helps to explain a few seemingly obscure sections of the main poem. Henry was seen during his brief life as something of a great Protestant hope against the generally Roman Catholic tendencies of the Stuarts. Trevelyan relates the tale that "Henry, Prince of Wales, who died in 1612, had told his father when he proposed to him a French marriage, that he was 'resolved that two religions should not lie in his bed.' If he had lived he might possibly have become a Protestant Henry V on the continent during the Thirty Years' War, and totally changed the course of political development in England. . . ."[7]

As we have seen from the allegorizing of the Roman Catholic church in *The Transformed Metamorphosis* and the continental Catholic courts in *The Revenger's Tragedy* and *The Atheist's Tragedy*, Tourneur was a militant Protestant—or at any rate, like most of his countrymen, a militant anti-Catholic. For a farsighted defender of the Anglican church, the death of Henry and the consequent elevation of Charles were bad news—although just how bad, only hindsight reveals.

Assuming that *A Grief on the Death of Prince Henry* reflects some fear of a Roman Catholic succession, it becomes clearer why the poem begins as it does. It is, to say the least, unconventional to begin an elegy as this one begins:

> Look up and see!
> And wonder to behold it. Some there be,
> That weepe not; but are strangely merrie, dance,
> And revell.
>
> (1–4)

These grotesque and evil antimourners may be those who rejoice in the loss of a Protestant heir—that is, those who favor a Catholic succession. It is also possible that the shadow of that succession may have been on Tourneur's mind when he described Henry's death as the first sign of a great, new plague.

The sense of personal, political, and religious implications of the death of the prince gives to Tourneur's "Grief" something of a less formal flavor than it might have upon first reading. So, too, does the repeated motif of the mourning of soldiers and scholars. One need not plumb too deeply into Tourneur's biography to realize that he himself was devoted to these two callings. Although the figure is a formal and appropriate one, its personal appropriateness suggests a poet whose "grief" is not simply a mechanical writing task.

Further, *A Grief on the Death of Prince Henry* is interesting in its suggestion of the company Tourneur may have kept as a working dramatist. Nicoll suggests that the tripartite publishing venture "indicates a bond of friendship and intimacy among the writers of what are in all probability the three greatest and most powerful plays of the age outside those of Shakespeare—*The Revenger's Tragedy, The White Devil,* and *A Woman Killed with Kindness.*"[8] While the collaborative effort probably does not really prove Tourneur, Webster, and Heywood were intimate friends, it does imply a fairly close working relationship between the three dramatists. At any rate, the three elegies suggest that Tourneur was not without taste in his choice of collaborators.

A Grief on the Death of Prince Henry finally merits note as yet another working out of Tourneur's favorite theme. Given the occasion of the work, it is surprising how easily Tourneur once again molds his material into a study of virtue surrounded by evil. While the poem is no *The Atheist's Tragedy,* there are moments when the attitude toward the death of a virtuous man in the poem are reminiscent of Charlemont's sentiments as he leaps up to the scaffold. There is even, at the conclusion of the poem, a brief reminder of the resurrection motif of *The Transformed Metamorphosis,* a reminder for the Christian that the resurrected Christ is the model of the good man in an evil world:

> . . . goe forth in teares.
> Yet some of Joy too, mix'd with those of Greefe;
> That flow from apprehension of releefe.
> I see His Spirit turn'd into a starre;
> Whose influence makes that His owne vertues are
> Succeeded justlie.
>
> (130–35)

Tourneur's three late minor poems are portraits of military, diplomatic, and princely virtue. The dark world of *The Revenger's Tragedy* is seen in these poems as a contrasting context in which that virtue may shine more brightly. Tourneur ends his literary career as he began, a profound pessimist who nevertheless believes deeply in the potential for man's virtue and in the reality of his salvation.

CHAPTER 7

Conclusion

THERE are two procedures by which it is possible to assess an author's position in literary history. The first is an external judgment: To what extent did the man and his works influence his contemporaries and/or those who came later? The second procedure involves an intrinsic evaluation: Regardless of the extent of their influence, what is the internal merit of the works themselves? Legitimate literary history can only be achieved when both these criteria are employed. In the case of Cyril Tourneur, both external influence and internal merit can be accurately assessed.

I External Influence

The measuring of Cyril Tourneur's effects on his contemporaries and following generations of dramatic poets is not without its pitfalls. Perhaps the first to be encountered is Tourneur's nearly universal classification as a "non-Shakespearean Renaissance Dramatist." A combination of the facts of history and the whims of academic convenience have conspired to divide the English drama of the Elizabethan and Jacobean periods into two largely artificial categories. First, and foremost, there is Shakespeare. Then there are the lesser dramatists. In one sense, of course, this division is justified—any dramatist is "secondary" to Shakespeare. In another sense, however, the split is neither real (Shakespeare and his fellow dramatists did not make it) nor useful. Had there been no Shakespeare, the English Renaissance would still have far outclassed any other period in our history in both quality and quantity within the genre of the drama. Thus, the "secondary" non-Shakespearean Renaissance dramatists in fact rank with the best our stage has ever offered. On the basis of *The Revenger's Tragedy* and *The Atheist's Tragedy* Tourneur, in turn, ranks high among his non-Shakespearean fellows.

140

Given the fact that Tourneur and most of his contemporaries are today studied under the shadow of the greatest master our literary tradition has produced, how do we discuss Tourneur's place within that tradition? One means of making this sort of evaluative judgment might be to consider Tourneur's influence upon subsequent theatrical work. Again, there is a difficulty, in that the theaters were closed less than twenty years after Tourneur's death, and reopened a generation later under re-formed, clearly non-Renaissance sorts of influences. On the basis of the Restoration alone, we would have to conclude that Beaumont and Fletcher exerted a far greater influence on the drama than did Shakespeare![1]

Notwithstanding Puritan incursions into literarary history, Tourneur did make a fairly significant contribution to the English stage. It was a negative contribution, but a real one nonetheless. As one surveys the history of the Jacobean stage, it seems clear that it was Tourneur, more than any other dramatist, who delivered the *coup de grâce* to one of the most fertile subgenres of our literature, the revenge tragedy. This form, within which was created Hamlet, surely one of the greatest plays of our culture, was never really taken seriously after *The Revenger's Tragedy* and *The Atheist's Tragedy*. After Tourneur, the revenge tragedy became the revenge melodrama or the revenge spectacle, a form which still lives today in the cheap and violent horse-operas of movies and television. But not since Tourneur has there been a serious movement which considered revenge an ethically justifiable dramatic motivation for violent action.

There can be no doubt that the revenge tragedy was dying when Tourneur wrote his plays, and it may well have died a natural death about when it did regardless of whether *The Revenger's Tragedy* and *The Atheist's Tragedy* had been written or not. The fact is that Tourneur put an end to a whole ethical complex in dramatic literature by conclusively demonstrating the moral inadequacies of that complex. After Tourneur's tragedies there could only come a movie actor like Clint Eastwood, with his bloody melodramas of unthinking vengeance—never again Hamlet.

II *Internal Values*

The ultimate value and importance of a literary artist, however, lies not so much in the external effects of his works, but in their internal merit. We must finally evaluate Tourneur by evaluating his

poems and plays, in and of themselves, as works of art. This task is
made easier by the fact that, taken together, Tourneur's works seem
to follow a meaningful pattern and to add up, in their totality, to a
coherent whole.

  The Transformed Metamorphosis introduces, in several ways, this
body of work. It is undeniably a youthful effort. Its theme is confused, and with a kind of garish appropriateness, its style echoes and
intensifies the confusion. Nevertheless, beneath the superficial
chaos of its theme and style, *The Transformed Metamorphosis* shows
Tourneur beginning to come to grips with the two parallel thematic
threads which were to run much more tightly through the remainder of his works. Here we find, in a modishly allegorized form,
Tourneur's first vision of a world fallen from its God-given beauty
into the darkness of decay and corruption. The darkness-and-light
imagery of the poem is almost compulsive in its revelation of the
fallen world. *All* is dark. To the extent that the world of *The Transformed Metamorphosis* is visible at all, it is seen through the weak,
flickering, evil light of sputtering torches, transformed and dark
stars, and bloody fires. This vision of a dark world overwhelms the
fashionable form of *The Transformed Metamorphosis*—it is too
strong to be restrained within the allegorical poetic formula the
young Tourneur picked to express it. As a result, the poem pos-
sesses a single-minded sense of oppression and gloom which make it
a more interesting work than it might have been had it been more
restrained and "successful."

  Coupled with this bleak and obsessive vision of a decaying world
is Tourneur's other thematic preoccupation, the saviour figure, the
man of virtue surrounded by and struggling against vice. Mavortio
seems, beneath his allegorical armor, half man, half God (and,
hence, a Christ figure). In his later, major works, Tourneur would
carefully separate the human and divine responses to a universe
charged with sin, rejecting the former to the extent that it was
independent of the latter. In *The Transformed Metamorphosis*,
however, there seems only to be some inchoate desire on the poet's
part to balance the downward pull of the fallen world with some
force for salvation. As a consequence, Mavortio is never sufficiently
explained, and he emerges as an unconvincing and ultimately unsatisfactory saviour figure. But the very unproductive ambiguity of
Mavortio asks the questions that Tourneur would attempt to answer
in his later, better works. How are redemption, virtue, and justice

to be brought into an evil world? What is the role of man, and what of God, in the search for salvation within a damned universe? The raising of these questions makes *The Transformed Metamorphosis* a fitting and stimulating poetic introduction to the dramatic works of Cyril Tourneur.

By far the strongest image which remains with the reader of *The Transformed Metamorphosis* is that of a dark and evil world. That world is the setting of *The Revenger's Tragedy*. It remains a pit of blackness—even the imagery of the play, like that of *The Transformed Metamorphosis*, depends heavily upon sharp contrasts between oppressive darkness and occupational flashes of fire. The fallen world of *The Revenger's Tragedy* however, is presented as both fuller and closer to the real world. By dropping much of the allegorical clumsiness of the earlier work (while retaining the atmosphere of a morality play). Tourneur makes the environs of *The Revenger's Tragedy* a convincing mirror of a degenerate society.

The Revenger's Tragedy suggests—in a far more specific, detailed, and, hence, convincing way than *The Transformed Metamorphosis*—a universe in which several "natures" are operating simultaneously. These "natures" are all more or less evil. The first and in some ways most vicious "nature" is human nature. The cast of characters of *The Revenger's Tragedy* is like a list of the variations of human depravity. Lust, ambition, cruelty, theft: all are there. Even the virtuous few finally lapse into evil. Vindice, who makes the fatal error of trusting his own nature, finds that it leads him as surely into sin as the Duke, the Duchess, Ambitioso, Supervacuo, Lussurioso, and the rest.

Coupled with vicious human nature is the material "natural" world, which expresses itself in a similar impulse toward decay. The central symbol of the play, the skull of Gloriana, is a constant *memento mori* or reminder of that process by which the human body decays into its component parts. Vindice (and to a lesser extent, the rest of the play's characters), with reminders from the skull, continually suggests the degenerative process of material nature. The mechanical laws of the universe of *The Revenger's Tragedy* are laws of mutability with a particularly nasty twist. As human nature tends toward sin, material nature moves to death and decay.

A third force operates in *The Revenger's Tragedy*. The play presents some sort of moral or spiritual order or power which is much more difficult to define than human or material nature. This power at times seems benevolent—as in the conversion of Gratiana. The name "Gratiana" and the process of her conversion suggest a divine grace capable of rescuing virtue in the right circumstances.

On the other hand, the supernatural power of *The Revenger's Tragedy* seems at other times almost a malevolent force. It is a moral force which is far more effective in destroying the evil—by making them destroy themselves—than in saving the good. This baleful force manifests itself in the overwhelming irony of *The Revenger's Tragedy*. Events are always twisted in such a way as to produce the opposite consequence from that their agents intended.

But friendly or terrible, it is this third order, above the human and the material, that clearly emerges the victor in *The Revenger's Tragedy*. In a sense, the real antagonists of the drama are Vindice and God. For Tourneur creates a universe in which a human being actively attempting to create justice makes himself the enemy of the divine. Vindice—and the whole ethic of human justice through revenge which he personifies—is tragically in error. He usurps the role of the heavens, and like a Greek tragic hero, he is damned for the usurpation. In *The Revenger's Tragedy* we encounter the same thematic elements as in *The Transformed Metamorphosis:* an evil world, human potential, divine intervention. But here these problems are separated and analyzed with far more precision, on a larger canvas. The flaws of the easy solution of *The Transformed Metamorphosis* are mercilessly exposed and the hopelessness of human action in attempting to save even a part of a fallen world is clearly revealed. Some clue to the solution of this problematic situation (the solution of *The Atheist's Tragedy*) is found in the characters of Gratiana, who seems saved by Grace, and old lord Antonio. Antonio, who has equal and similar cause for revenge with Vindice, is introduced early in the play, reappears occasionally, and at the conclusion is suddenly capitulated into a position of great power, his revenge having been accomplished for him without any action on his part. Although some readers of *The Revenger's Tragedy* find suggestions of cynicism and cunning on the part of Antonio, most see him as a prefiguration of the patient, "honest" men of *The Atheist's Tragedy*.

In *The Transformed Metamorphosis*, Mavortio suggested a solution, but what remains with the reader is the problem. In *The Revenger's Tragedy*, Antonio and Gratiana suggest the right solution, but what dominates the play is Vindice and his wrong solution.

The play chronicles the total inadequacy of "self reliant" human beings to deal with a corrupted world.

In *The Atheist's Tragedy*, the three worlds of *The Revenger's Tragedy* are more clearly defined, more perfectly balanced. Humanity and human nature remain a weak and fallible force. The play's characters are either evil (D'amville, Levidulcia), weak (Roussard), or demonstrably susceptible to temptation. Sebastian, the man of "good nature," falls to the status of victim of a particularly low plot. Even Charlemont has to learn—after some serious mistakes—that his own impulses are not to be trusted.

Physical nature is an even more important aspect of *The Atheist's Tragedy* than human nature, and like it, is corrupted and corrupting. Indeed, the play is easily seen as a thesis work, denying D'amville's carefully expressed naturalistic philosophy. Men have an impulse—which only God can thwart—to become animals, Tourneur suggests. Thus, the believer in nature condemns himself to the zoo. One may go to the route of impulse and sensuality, as does Levidulcia, or choose philosphy and reason with D'amville: it makes no difference. The person who puts his faith in either the nature of man or the world of material nature is doomed. Like D'amville's dreams of a great house, such a person is constructing a life based on weak or no foundations, and all that will soon remain will be a pile of unidentifiable rubble.

In *The Atheist's Tragedy*, however, the solution that Tourneur had groped toward in *The Transformed Metamorphosis* and hinted at in *The Revenger's Tragedy* is at last fully developed. Given the degeneration of human and material nature, the only possiblity for a successful life lies in resignation to a higher order. That spiritual power which manifested itself largely as a destroyer of evil in *The Revenger's Tragedy* is here a more important and more precisely defined force. The movement seems to have been from generalized mythology (Mavortio) through a negative moral order (the irony of *The Revenger's Tragedy*) to God. The God of *The Atheist's Tragedy* is seen through myth—Charlemont, for example, "dies" and returns from the dead, an echo of the resurrection motif of *The Transformed Metamorphosis*, and more clearly an echo of the basic Christian theme of resurrection. The God of *The Atheist's Tragedy* certainly retains the ironic power to hoist evil by its own petard so important to the development of *The Revenger's Tragedy*. But in the latter play, and not the earlier, God also has the power and the inclination to move directly in the world of man and shower mercy and grace upon those who put their faith in Him. Charlemont and Castabella are erring human beings, like most of the rest of Tourneur's characters. But they know they are *only* erring human beings, and Tourneur gives to them a clear awareness of a world beyond their own which permits them to transcend their errors. Their faith gives them the courage to face death with ease, the sensitivity and generosity to love each other, and the patience to be happy.

The personal qualities which can be won only through faith are illustrated in Tourneur's three late minor poems. Each illustrates some specific or generalized virtues of character in its subject. The "Funeral Poem" commemorates the courage and intelligence of an ideal soldier. The "Character" shows the selflessness, pragmatism, and wit of an ideal diplomat and counselor. The "Grief" eulogizes an ideal Protestant prince.

Tourneur's works, then, are the chronicle of an evolving Christian pessimism. The bass chord which rumbles through them all is a deep distrust of man and his physical universe. The developing countertheme is one of belief in a world above man and nature which offers a hope of salvation.

Notes and References

Preface

1. Robert Ornstein, *The Moral Vision of Jacobean Tragedy* (Madison, Wis. 1960), p. 112.

Chapter One

1. The spelling of the name as "Cyril Tourneur" is the accepted modern practice. In the Renaissance, "Tourneur" like "Shakespeare" was written a number of ways: "Turner," "Tourneur," "Turnor," are common. "Cyril" also appears in several variations, including "Cyrill" and two odd spellings, which are perhaps copyists' errors, "Jerill" and "Will." "Tourneur," as the variant spellings suggest, is pronounced "Turner."

2. *The Works of Cyril Tourneur*, ed., Allardyce Nicoll (London, 1929; reprint, New York, 1963), p. 8. All quotations from Tourneur's works are from this edition, hereafter cited as Nicoll.

3. The "Character" is an extinct literary form, quite popular in the Renaissance. It consists of a short prose description of a person, either real (for example, Tourneur's "Character of Robert, Earl of Salisbury") or typical (for example, "A Merchant").

4. The Middle Temple was one of the Inns of Court, an English institution somewhere between a law school and a dormitory for aristocratic young Londoners. The Inns of Court are important in the history of the English drama, because the young men connected with them were theater fans. Many Renaissance plays were written for, and/or performed in, the Inns of Court.

5. Neville Williams, *Henry VIII and His Court* (New York, 1971), p. 173.

6. G. M. Trevelyan, *History of England* (London, 1926; reprint, Garden City, N.Y., 1953), II, 84.

7. This English navy was outfitted, in the 1580s, largely by Sir John Hawkins, who served as treasurer of the navy from 1578. Hawkins developed the English "galleon," designed to carry as many guns and as few men as far and as fast as possible. These superior ships, in the hands of a well-paid and well-trained naval force, proved invincible.

8. S. T. Bindoff, *Tudor England* (Baltimore, 1950), p. 270. This is also the source of the quotation in the next sentence.

9. Ibid., p. 277

10. *The Dictionary of National Biography*, eds., Leslie Stephen and Sidney Lee (London, 1917), XX, 230.

11. Peter Murray, *A Study of Cyril Tourneur* (Philadelphia, 1964), p. 18.

12. Bindoff, *Tudor England*, p. 277.

13. C. R. Markham, *The Fighting Veres* (New York, 1888), p. 109.

14. The official registry of the Stationers' Company, the monopolistic printing guild which controlled, by royal character, the making of books from 1557 through the seventeenth century. Since only the members of the company could make books, and since all books made by members of the company had to be registered, the Stationers' Register is an invaluable source of sixteenth- and seventeenth-century bibliographical information.

15. Nicoll, p. 23. This problem is also discussed, quite lucidly, by T. S. Eliot in his essay, "Cyril Tourneur," in *Essays on Elizabethan Drama* (London, 1932; reprint, New York, 1960), pp. 115–17.

16. E. K. Chambers, *The Elizabethan Stage* (Oxford, 1923), III, 500; IV, 126–27. This fragment is printed in Nicoll, pp. 257–58.

17. Nicoll, p. 28 quotes W. W. Greg's *The Henslowe Papers*, pp. 72, 75.

18. Chambers, *The Elizabethan Stage*, I, 371.

19. Ibid., I, 375.

20. Ibid., I, 374.

21. G. Davies, *The Early Stuarts 1603–1660* (Oxford, 1937) p. 46.

22. J. R. Jones, *Britain and Europe in the Seventeenth Century* (New York, 1966), p. 19.

23. Davies, *The Early Stuarts*, p. 56.

24. L. B. Smith, "England's Second Family," *Horizon* 9 (Autumn, 1967), p. 69.

25. Davies, *The Early Stuarts*, p. 2.

26. *Dictionary of National Biography*, III, 1304.

27. Quoted from Murray, *A Study of Cyril Tourneur*, pp. 18–19.

28. Both quotations from *The Acts of the Privy Council* are found in Nicoll, p. 29.

29. Much of our information concerning the last phases of Tourneur's life is provided by a letter written by his widow, Mary, complaining to the privy council that she had not received her late husband's pension. The letter (written in 1632) is quoted in full in Nicoll, p. 31. It sets forth in some detail the history and nature of Tourneur's position under Cecil at and before the Cadiz expedition. It is, as noted earlier, the first and last indication that Tourneur was married:

Chapter Two

1. Ben Jonson, *Three Plays* (New York, 1961), p. 5.

2. John Webster, *Complete Works*, ed. F. L. Lucas (London, 1927), I, 107.

3. The metaphor is reminiscent of Chaucer's Troilus.

4. Nicoll, p. 11.

5. Hallett Smith, *Elizabethan Poetry* (Cambridge, 1952), p. 194.

6. Ibid., p. 206.

7. This anti-church posture—be it a generalized antiinstitutionalism or specific anti-Catholicism—figures importantly in *The Atheist's Tragedy*, an otherwise conservative work in questions of religion.

8. D. Pym, "A Theory on the Identification of Cyril Tourneur's 'Mavortio,'" *Notes and Queries* 179 (1938), 201, 204; A. C. Hamilton, "Spenser and Tourneur's *Transformed Metamorphosis*," *Review of English Studies* 8 (1957), 127–36.

9. E. M. W. Tillyard, *The Elizabethan World Picture* (London, 1943).

10. T. S. Eliot, *Essays on Elizabethan Drama*, p. 119.

11. *The Plays and Poems of Cyril Tourneur*, ed. John Churton Collins, II, (London, 1878), 222–31.

12. Nicoll, p. 12.

13. Nicoll, p. 15.

14. See, for example, Samuel Schoenbaum, *Shakespeare's Lives* (Evanston, Ill, 1970).

15. Pym, "A Theory on the Identification of Cyril Tourneur's 'Mavortio,'" p. 202.

16. Ibid., p. 204

17. Kenneth N. Cameron, "Cyril Tourneur and *The Transformed Metamorphosis*," *Review of English Studies* 16 (1940), 24.

18. Ibid.

19. Ibid.

20. John D. Peter, "The Identity of Mavortio in Tourneur's *The Transformed Metamorphosis*," *Notes and Queries* 193 (1948) 408–12.

21. Ibid., p. 411.

22. Murray, *A Study of Cyril Tourneur.*

23. Ibid., p. 26

24. Ibid., p. 30.

25. Readers who wish to explore this pattern in greater depth are urgeds to familiarize themselves with the Cambridge anthropologists of myth, especially Sir James Frazier, and the literary myth critics, especially Northerop Frye.

26. For example, Mircea Eliade, *Patterns in Comparative Religion*, (Cleveland, 1963).

27. The question of the authorship of *Laugh and Lie Down* is taken up in Chapter 1.

28. *The Works of Geoffrey Chaucer*, ed. F. N. Robinson (Cambridge, 1957), p. 310.

29. The connection cited here must remain tenuous—many ballads were simply part of the commonplace oral traditions of the times, and many more were no doubt printed as broadsides, then lost.

Chapter Three

1. Both lists are printed in W. W. Greg, *A List of English Plays Written Before 1643 and Printed Before 1700* (London, 1900), Appendix 2. The first was appended to *The Old Law*, the second to *Tom Tyler and His Wife*, and revised and added to *Nicomede*.

2. See S. Schoenbaum, *Internal Evidence and Elizabethan Dramatic Authorship* (Evanston, Ill., 1966), for a much fuller and more balanced treatment of this period.

3. Felix Schelling, *Elizabethan Drama* (New York, 1908), vol. II, pt. 1, 568. For other similar exemplary early doubters, see Paul Wenzel, *Cyril Tourneurs Stellung in der Geshicte des englischen Dramas* (Breslau, 1918), and Ashley Thorndike, *Tragedy* (Boston, 1905).

4. *A Biographical Chronicle of the English Drama, 1559–1642* (London, 1891), II, 264, 272, 272. Throughout the remainder of the footnotes for this chapter the practice of citing with one footnote several adjacent quotations when clearly identified in the text as coming from one source has been adopted.

5. E. H. C. Oliphant, "Problems of Authorship in Elizabethan Dramatic Literature," *Modern Philology* 8 (1910–1911), 427, 428.

6. H. Dugdale Sykes, "Cyril Tourneur: 'The Revenger's Tragedy' 'The Second Maiden's Tragedy', " *Notes and Queries*, 12th ser. 5 (1919), 227, 226, 225.

7. E. H. C. Oliphant, "The Authorship of *The Revenger's Tragedy*," *Studies in Philology* 23 (1926), 157–58, 159, 160, 161, 168.

8. Nicoll, pp. 19, 21.

9. Allardyce Nicoll, "*The Revenger's Tragedy* and the Virtue of Anonymity," in *Essays on Shakespeare and the Elizabethan Drama in Honor of Hardin Craig* (Columbia, 1962), 309–16.

10. This essay, "Cyril Tourneur," first appeared in the *Times Literary Supplement* of November 13, 1930, and was reprinted in Eliot's *Selected Essays* and in *Essays on Elizabethan Drama* ([New York, 1956], pp. 110–24). The citations are from this last edition, pp. 113 and 112.

11. E. H. C. Oliphant, "Tourneur and *The Revenger's Tragedy*," *Times Literary Supplement*, December 18, 1930, p. 1087.

12. T. S. Eliot, "Tourneur and *The Revenger's Tragedy*," *Times Literary Supplement*, January 1, 1931, p. 12.

13. B. M. Wagner, "Cyril Tourneur," *Times Literary Supplement*, April 23, 1931, p. 327.

14. F. L. Jones, "Cyril Tourneur," *Times Literary Supplement*, June 18, 1931, p. 487.

15. E. H. C. Oliphant, "Tourneur and Mr. T. S. Eliot," *Studies in Philology* 32 (1955), 547, 550.

16. H. N. Hillebrand, "Thomas Middleton's 'The Viper's Brood,' " *Modern Language Notes* 42 (1927), 35–38.

17. W. P. Dunkel, "The Authorship of *The Revenger's Tragedy*," *Publications of the Modern Language Association* XLVI (1931), 785.

18. U. M. Ellis-Fermor, "The Imagery of *The Revenger's Tragedy* and *The Atheists' Tragedy*," *Modern Language Review* 30, no. 3 (1935), 292.

19. Marco K. Mincoff, "The Authorship of *The Revenger's Tragedy*," *Studia Historico-Philologica Serdincensia* 2 (1940), 5, 10, 40, 2.

20. Inga-Stina Ekeblad, "An Approach to Tourneur's Imagery," *Modern Language Review* 59 (1959), 489, 492, 496, 498.

21. L. G. Salingar, "*The Revenger's Tragedy* and the Morality Tradition," *Scrutiny* 6 (March, 1938), 402–24; reprinted in R. J. Kaufman, ed., *Elizabethan Drama: Modern Essays in Criticism* (New York, 1961), 208–24.

23. T. M. Parrott and R. H. Ball, *A Short View of Elizabethan Drama* (New York, 1943), pp. 218, 216.

24. H. H. Adams, "Cyril Tourneur on Revenge," *Journal of English and Germanic Philology* 48 (1949), 72, 78, 79, 87.

25. Samuel Schoenbaum, "*The Revenger's Tragedy* and Middleton's Moral Outlook," Notes and Queries 196 (January, 1951), 9, 10.

26. R. A. Foakes, "On the Authorship of *The Revenger's Tragedy*," *Modern Language Review* 48 (1953), 136.

27. Robert Ornstein, "The Ethical Design of *The Revenger's Tragedy*," *English Literary History* 21, no. 2 (1954), 91.

28. Robert Ornstein, *The Moral Vision of Jacobean Tragedy* (Madison, Wisc. 1960).

29. J. D. Peter, "*The Revenger's Tragedy* Reconsidered," *Essays in Criticism* 6, no. 2 (1956), 134, 139.

30. J. D. Peter, *Complaint and Satire in Early English Literature* (Oxford, 1956, pp. 273–82.

31. Inga-Stina Ekeblad, "On the Authorship of *The Revenger's Tragedy*," *English Studies* 41 (1960), 227, 236.

32. Irving Ribner, *Jacobean Tragedy* (London, 1962), p. 72.

33. *The Atheist's Tragedy*, ed. Irving Ribner (Cambridge, 1962, p. lil.

34. Inga-Stina Ekeblad, "A Note on *The Revenger's Tragedy*," *Notes and Queries* 200 (1955), 98.

35. *The Revenger's Tragedy*, ed. R. A. Foakes (Cambridge, 1966), p. liii.

36. R. H. Barker, "The Authorship of *The Second Maiden's Tragedy* and *The Revenger's Tragedy*," *Shakespeare Association Bulletin* 20 (1945), 126.

37. R. H. Barker, *Thomas Middleton* (New York, 1958), p. 70.

38. Samuel Schoenbaum, *Middleton's Tragedies* (New York, 1955), pp. 82.

39. M. P. Jackson, "Affirmative Particles in *Henry VIII*," *Notes and*

Queries 207 (1962), 374. The historian and linguist is tempted to reply, "Oh yeah?"

40. Murray, *A Study of Cyril Tourneur*, p. 145.

41. George R. Price, "The Authorship and the Bibliography of *The Revenger's Tragedy*," *The Library*, 5th Ser. 15 (1960), 265.

42. Samuel Schoenbaum, *Internal Evidence and Elizabethan Dramatic Authorship* (Evanston, Ill. 1966). This book is a greatly expanded version of "Internal Evidence and the Attribution of Elizabethan Plays," *Bulletin of the New York Public Library* 65 (1961), 102–24; reprinted, unfortunately with most of the discussion of *The Revenger's Tragedy* deleted, in Erdman and Fogle, eds., *Evidence for Authorship* (1966), 188–203.

43. Allardyce Nicoll, "*The Revenger's Tragedy* and the Virtue of Anonymity," p. 309.

44. *The Revenger's Tragedy*, ed. Lawrence J. Ross, p. xviii.

45. Alfred Harbage and Samuel Schoenbaum, *The Annals of English Drama* (London, 1964).

Chapter Four

1. C. V. Boyer, *The Villain as Hero in Elizabethan Tragedy* (New York, 1914), p. 145.

2. C. F. T. Brooke, *The Tudor Drama* (Boston, 1911), pp. 445, 220. See also, for expressions of the same attitude, F. S. Boas, *An Introduction to Stuart Drama* (Oxford, 1946); M. Doran, *Endeavors of Art* (Madison, Wisc. 1954); J. A. Symonds, *Webster and Tourneur* New York, 1956); R.C. Harrier, ed., *Jacobean Drama* New York, 1963), vol. II, Introduction; H. Jenkins, "Cyril Tourneur," *Review of English Studies* (1941), 21–36; C. Lamb, *Specimens of the English Dramatic Poets* (London, 1908); Moody Prior, *The Language of Tragedy* (Chicago, 1947); A. D. Rossiter, *English Drama from Early Times to the Elizabethans* (London, 1950); F. Schelling, *Elizabethan Drama* (New York, 1908); R. B. Sharpe, *Irony in the Drama* (Chapel Hill, 1959); C. E. Vaughan, et al., eds., *The Cambridge History of English Literature* (New York, 1910), 188–211; H. W. Wells, *Elizabethan and Jacobean Playwrights* (New York, 1939).

3. *The Jacobean Drama*, p. 155.

4. "Cyril Tourneur," in *Selected Essays*, p. 120. See also Murray, *A Study of Cyril Tourneur*, p. 190. The case is also ably argued in J. D. Peter's "*The Revenger's Tragedy* Reconsidered," and an interesting compromise is offered in T. B. Tomlinson's *A Study of Elizabethan and Jacobean Playwrights* Cambridge, 1964): Tourneur tends "to gloat over the thing he condemns" (p. 105).

5. Schoenbaum, *Middleton's Tragedies*, p. 6.

6. N. W. Bawcutt, "*The Revenger's Tragedy* and the Medici Family," *Notes and Queries* 202 (1957), 192–93; S. Schoenbaum, "*The Revenger's Tragedy*: A Neglected Source," *Notes and Queries* 195 (1950), 338; L. G.

Salingar, *"The Revenger's Tragedy:* Some Possible Sources," *Modern Language Review* 55 (1965), 3–12.

7. Murray, *A Study of Cyril Tourneur,* p. 197.

8. Schoenbaum, *Middleton's Tragedies,* p. 8.

9. Ornstein, *The Moral Vision of Jacobean Tragedy,* p. 107.

10. Schoenbaum, *Middleton's Tragedies,* p. 28.

11. Ekeblad, "An Approach to Tourneur's Imagery," p. 489. See Also L. G. Salingar, *"The Revenger's Tragedy* and the Morality Tradition."

12. Ribner, *Jacobean Tragedy,* p. 8.

13. Ornstein, "The Ethical Design of *The Revenger's Tragedy,"* p. 91.

14. Murray, *A Study of Cyril Tourneur,* p. 205.

15. P. Lisca, *"The Revenger's Tragedy:* A Study in Irony," *Philological Quarterly* 38 (1959), 242–51; reprinted in *Shakespeare's Contemporaries,* ed. M. Bluestone and N. Rabkin (Englewood Cliffs, N.J., 1970), p. 310.

16. For example, H. H. Adams, "Cyril Tourneur on Revenge," *Journal of English and Germanic Philology* 48 (1949), 72–87; F. T. Bowers, *Elizabethan Revenge Tragedy, 1587–1642* (Princeton, N.J., 1940); L. G. Salingar, "Tourneur and the Tragedy of Revenge," in *The Age of Shakespeare,* ed. B. Ford (New York, 1955), 334–54.

17. Bowers, *Elizabethan Revenge Tragedy,* p. 133. See also A. Kernan, *The Cankered Muse* (New Haven, Conn., 1959).

18. For a fuller discussion see my "The Ring and the Jewel in Webster's Tragedies," *Texas Studies in Literature and Language* 14 (1972), 253–68.

19. J. W. Lever, ed., *Every Man in His Humor* by Ben Jonson, (Lincoln, Neb., 1971), p. xxi.

20. Murray, *A Study of Cyril Tourneur,* p. 190.

21. J. W. Lever, *The Tragedy of State* (London, 1971), p. 4.

22. Ibid., pp. 330–31.

23. Ribner, *Jacobean Tragedy,* p. 72.

24. Schoenbaum, *Middleton's Tragedies,* p. 29; Foakes, Introduction to *The Revenger's Tragedy,* p. xxii.

25. Samuel Schoenbaum, *"The Revenger's Tragedy:* Jacobean Dance of Death," *Modern Langauge Quarterly* 15 (1954), 207.

26. (Leyden, 1586), p. 229b.

27. Foakes, Introduction to *The Revenger's Tragedy,* pp. xxxviii, xxxix, xxix.

28. Schoenbaum, *Middleton's Tragedies,* p. 23.

29. Foakes, Introduction to *The Revenger's Tragedy,* p. xxx.

30. Parrott and Ball, *A Short View of Elizabethan Drama,* p. 222.

31. Ekeblad, "An Approach to Tourneur's Imagery," p. 496.

32. Ellis-Fermor, "The Imagery of *The Revenger's Tragedy* and The Atheist's Tragedy," p. 292.

33. Schoenbaum, *Middleton's Tragedies,* p. 25; A. C. Swinburne, *Works,* eds. Gosse and Wise, XI, 473.

34. Parrott and Ball, *A Short View of Elizabethan Drama,* pp. 221–22.

Chapter Five

1. Ellis-Fermor, *Jacobean Drama*, p. 164.

2. Schoenbaum, *Middleton's Tragedies*, p. 162.

3. Nicoll, Introduction, pp. 39–40.

4. R. Ornstein, "The Atheist's Tragedy and Renaissance Naturalism," *Studies in Philology* 51 (1954), 195. See also I. Ribner, ed., *The Atheist's Tragedy*, Introduction, p. xxxix and T. Spencer, *Death and Elizabethan Tragedy*, (Cambridge, Mass., 1936), p. 123.

5. Ribner, Introduction to *The Atheist's Tragedy*, p. 2.

6. Murray, *A Study of Cyril Tourneur*, p. 92. See also R. Levin, "The Subplot of *The Atheist's Tragedy*," *Huntington Library Quarterly* 29 (1965), 17–33.

7. In this speech D'amville again rejects the notion, here presented in astrological terms, that a higher power controls the world through nature. See J. M. S. Tompkins, "Tourneur and the Stars," *Review of English Studies* 22 (1946), 315–19. This scene, and others like it, probably all owe much to that first and greatest atheist and materialist of the English Renaissance drama, Marlowe's Faustus, who first appears alone and soliloquizing in his study as the play opens. See also Marlowe's *The Jew of Malta*, I. i. 37 for "infinite riches in a little room." The quotation from Volpone which follows is from *Jonson, Three Plays*, eds. Nicholson and Herford (New York, 1957), I, 1–112.

8. Murray, *A Study of Cyril Tourneur*, p. 98 and Ornstein, *The Moral Vision of Jacobean Tragedy*, p. 119.

9. Murray, *A Study of Cyril Tourneur*, p. 91. See also Levin, "The Subplot of *The Atheist's Tragedy*," p. 23.

10. Parrott and Ball, *A Short View of Elizabethan Drama*, p. 221.

11. Levin, "The Subplot of *The Atheist's Tragedy*," p. 23.

12. Murray, *A Study of Cyril Tourneur*.

13. Levin, "The Subplot of *The Atheist's Tragedy*," p. 23.

14. Doran, *Endeavors of Art*. p. 357.

15. Eliot, "Cyril Tourneur," pp. 119, 116.

16. Doran, *Endeavors of Art*, p. 352.

17. Ribner, Introduction to *The Atheist's Tragedy*, p. li. For the theory that the work is a compromise between literary revenge traditions and religious scruples, see Bowers, *Elizabethan Revenge Tragedy*, p. 185.

18. Jenkins, "Cyril Tourneur," pp. 21–22.

19. Ellis-Fermor, *Jacobean Drama*, p. 156. See also M. H. Higgins, "The Influence of Calvinistic Thought in *The Atheist's Tragedy*," *Review of English Studies* 19 (1943), 255–62.

20. Schoenbaum, *Middleton's Tragedies*, p. 164.

21. Eliot, "Cyril Tourneur," p. 119.

22. Ekblad, "An Approach to Tourneur's Imagery," p. 490.

23. Foakes, "On the Authorship of *The Revenger's Tragedy*," p. 138 and Ellis-Fermor, *The Jacobean Drama*, p. 161.

24. Ekeblad, "An Appraoch to Tourneur's Imagery," p. 491.

25. Ellis-Fermor, "The Imagery of *The Revenger's Tragedy* and *The Atheist's Tragedy*," p. 290.

26. Murray, *A Study of Cyril Tourneur*, p. 111. Murray discusses both patterns of imagery at greater length.

27. Ibid., p. 115

28. Perhaps, as Murray suggests, related to the legends of St. Winifrid, at the site of whose martyrdom a miraculous pure stream was created. The churchyard in which most of Act 4 takes place is attached to a church of St. Winifrid.

29. Murray, *A Study of Cyril Tourneur*, p. 129.

30. Tompkins, "Tourneur and the Stars," p. 318.

31. C. Leech, "*The Atheist's Tragedy* as a Dramatic Comment on Chapman's *Bussy* Plays," *Journal of English and Germanic Philology* 52 (1953), 526, 528, 530.

32. Ribner, Introduction to *The Atheist's Tragedy*, pp. lxiii–lxiv. See also the notes of this edition for a detailed annotation of the multiple uses of *King Lear* in *The Atheist's Tragedy*.

Chapter Six

1. See Murray, *A Study of Cyril Tourneur:* "The poem is important chiefly as it shows Tourneur's considerable familiarity with Vere's military career and with his methods as a commander . . . ." (p. 16); and Nicoll, "The chief intrest of *A Funerall Poeme* must rest in its historical significance. It seems certain that by this time at least Tourneur was in active association with those occupied in the campaigns of the Low Countries; and this fact gives additional warrant for believing that he may have been so associated even in the last years of the sixteenth century" (p. 22).

2. Murray, *A Study of Cyril Tourneur*, p. 16.

3. Nicoll, p. 22.

4. Parrott and Ball, *A Short View of the Elizabethan Drama*, p. 219.

5. Smith, "England's Second Family," p. 71.

6. Nicoll, p. 338.

7. Trevelyan, *History of England*, II, 163–64 n.

8. Nicoll, p. 27.

Chapter Seven

1. This judgment is based upon a determination of popularity measured by performances.

Selected Bibliography

PRIMARY SOURCES

1. Complete works
The Works of Cyril Tourneur. Edited by Allardyce Nicoll. London: The
Fanfrolico Press 1929; reprint, New York: Russell and Russell, 1963.
2. Specific Works
The Atheist's Tragedy. Edited by Irving Ribner. The Revels Plays. Cam-
bridge, Mass: Harvard University Press, 1964.
The Revenger's Tragedy. Edited by R. A. Foakes. The Revels Plays. Cam-
bridge, Mass: Harvard University Press, 1966.
The Revenger's Tragedy. Edited by Lawrence J. Ross. Regents Renaissance
Drama. Lincoln: University of Nebraska Press, 1966.

SECONDARY SOURCES

1. General works on Tourneur and Renaissance drama
ADAMS, HENRY H. "Cyril Tourneur on Revenge." *Journal of English and
Germanic Philology* 48 (1949), 72–87. A study of the developing con-
cept of the morality of revenge in the drama.
BOWERS, F. T. *Elizabethan Revenge Tragedy, 1587–1642.* Princeton:
Princeton University Press, 1940. Tourneur's plays, particularly *The
Revenger's Tragedy*, discussed within the context of the genre of the
revenge play.
BRADBOOK, M. C. *Themes and Conventions of Elizabethan Tragedy.* Cam-
bridge: Cambridge University Press, 1952. Notable for a discussion of
Tourneur's use of irony. Otherwise a rather spotty treatment of Tour-
neur.
EKEBLAD, INGA-STINA. "An Approach to Tourneur's Imagery." *Modern
Language Review* 54 (1959), 489–98. A discussion of the imagistic
techniques of *The Revenger's Tragedy* and *The Atheist's Tragedy*. Although the styles of imagery of the two plays are found to differ, images
in both are carefully chosen to convey a moral content.
ELIOT, T. S. *Essays on Elizabethan Drama.* New York: Harcourt Brace and
World, 1956. Particularly useful is the essay "Cyril Tourneur," which

was written as a review of Nicoll's edition of the *Works*, and also appeared in *Selected Essays* (1932). Although much of the essay deals with the questions of authorship and dating of *The Revenger's Tragedy* and *The Atheist's Tragedy*, it also contains valuable criticism. Eliot's view of Tourneur as obsessed with an adolescent and morbid preoccupation with death is germinal.

ELLIS-FERMOR, UNA. "The Imagery of *The Revenger's Tragedie* and *The Atheist's Tragedie.*" *Modern Language Review* 30 (1935), 289–301. A study of "image clusters" in the two works, particularly the image of the great house in *The Atheist's Tragedy*.

————. *The Jacobean Drama*. Rev. ed. London: Methuen, 1958. A general study in which Tourneur is presented as both a moralist and a careful workman who, nevertheless, sees the universe as unredeemably malignant.

JENKINS, HAROLD. "Cyril Tourneur." *Review of English Studies* 17 (1941), 21–36. This article is of particular historical interest in its almost complete identification of the author with his characters. Thus, *The Revenger's Tragedy* reveals a dramatist obsessed with a hatred of mankind, *The Atheist's Tragedy* ultimately rejects a naturalistic philosophy which may have once attracted Tourneur.

LEVER, J. W. *The Tragedy of State*. London: Methuen, 1971. An argument against those (For example, John Peter, Willard Farnham) who stress the medieval aspects of Renaissance drama. Lever sees the growing power of the state, not the continuing force of religion, as a dominant influence. Hence, *The Revenger's Tragedy* is discussed as a portrait of a perverted court,.

MURRAY, PETER. *A Study of Cyril Tourneur*. Philadelphia: University of Pennsylvania Press, 1964. While not perfect (a 30-page "proof" that *The Revenger's Tragedy* is not by Tourneur is followed by a 70-page discussion that presumes it is; no consideration of the minor works; hasty biography), this is clearly the major study of Tourneur to date. The critical discussions of both plays are enlightened, and the analysis of *The Transformed Metamorphosis* is scholarly and impressive.

ORNSTEIN, ROBERT. *The Moral Vision of Jacobean Tragedy*. Madison: University of Wisconsin Press, 1960. A valuable discussion of ten Jacobean tragedians, including Shakespeare, within the context suggested by the title. The treatment of Tourneur is noteworthy for the study of the use of Italy and the Italianate in *The Revenger's Tragedy* and a somewhat negative view of *The Atheist's Tragedy* (the subject of which, while suited to Tourneur's moralizing temper, Ornstein finds, was beyond his artistic capabilities).

PETER, JOHN. *Complaint and Satire in Early English Literature*. Oxford: Oxford University Press, 1956. Although what Peter says about Tourneur (here and elsewhere) is valuable, this work is particularly useful as a study of a type of literature which had a powerful effect upon the tragedies, *The Transformed Metamorphosis*, and *Laugh and Lie Down*. The satiric is, as Peter notes, a major element in Tourneur's work.

RIBNER, IRVING. *Jacobean Tragedy*. London; Baylis, 1962. Subtitled *The Quest for Moral Order*, Ribner's book suggests that a major direction in the works of six Jacobean dramatists—including Tourneur—is the attempt to impose an ethical design upon a world which was seen as descending into chaos. Ribner contends that Tourneur's approach to this situation was a return to "primitive Christianity."

TOMPKINS, J. M. S. "Tourneur and the Stars," *Review of English Studies* 16 (1940), 315–19. An interesting consideration of Tourneur's use of myth and image.

2. Studies of *The Transformed Metamorphosis*

CAMERON, K. N. "Cyril Tourneur and *The Transformed Metamorphosis*." *Review of English Studies* 16 (1940), 18–24. Cameron interprets the poem as a militant Protestant defense of Sir Christopher Heydon.

HAMILTON, A. C. "Spenser and Tourneur's *Transformed Metamorphosis*." *Review of English Studies*, n.s. 8 (1957), 127–36. Hamilton is concerned not only with the Spenserian imitation of the poem, but advances an identification of Mavortio as Spenser.

PETER, JOHN. "The identity of Mavortio in Tourneur's *Transformed Metamorphosis*." *Notes and Queries* 193 (1948), 408–12. A reading of the poem as a political allegory, with Mavortio identified as King Henry VIII (The Unicorn, of course, is Elizabeth.)

PYM, DOROTHY. "A Theory on the Identification of Cyril Tourneur's Mavortio." *Notes and Queries* 179 (1938), 201–4. Spenser, again.

3. Studies of *The Revenger's Tragedy*

BOYER, C. V. *The Villain as Hero in Elizabethan Tragedy*. 1914. Reprint, New York: Russell and Russell, 1964. While Boyer's comments about *The Revenger's Tragedy* are not particularly enlightening, his early study of the class of character to which Vindice belongs is important.

KERNAN, ALVIN. *The Cankered Muse*. New Haven: Yale University Press, 1959. The section on *The Revenger's Tragedy* is printed separately as "Tragical Satire and The Revenger's Tragedy," in *Shakespeare's Contemporaries*, edited by M. Bluestone and N. Rabkin ([Englewood Cliffs: Prentice Hall, 1970], pp. 317–29). An extremely valuable study of satire in general and in *The Revenger's Tragedy*. Vindice is discussed as not simply a character, but a satirist, commenting upon other characters and society.

LISCA, PETER. "*The Revenger's Tragedy*: A Study in Irony." *Philological Quarterly* 38 (1959), 242–51. Lisca sees the irony of the play as ubiquitous, based upon a Christian—perhaps Puritan—point of view, and an important unifying element within the drama.

MINCOFF, MARCO K. "The Authorship of *The Revenger's Tragedy*." *Studia*

Historico-Philogica Serdicensia 2 (1940), 1–87. An image study, attempting to prove that Tourneur was not the author of the play. Nevertheless, a careful and detailed explication of the compression, fertility, and power of the imagery of *The Revenger's Tragedy*.

OLIPHANT, E. H. C. "The Authorship of *The Revenger's Tragedy*." *Studies in Philology* 23 (1926), 157–68. A typical work by the most important of the critics who raised the possibility of Middleton's authorship.

SALINGAR, L. G. "Tourneur and the Tragedy of Revenge." In *The Age of Shakespeare*, edited by B. Ford, pp. 334–54. New York: Penguin, 1955. *The Revenger's Tragedy* as the last and one of the most powerful and passionate attempts to present moral problems within the genre of the revenge tragedy.

———. "*The Revenger's Tragedy* and the Morality Tradition." *Scrutiny* 6 (1938), 402–24. An important essay showing how the schematic manipulation of characters and events for purposes of moral didacticism makes the play similar to the morality plays.

SCHOENBAUM, S. *Middleton's Tragedies*, New York: Columbia University Press, 1955. The play, here attributed to Middleton, is brilliantly presented as a complex matrix of literary and theatrical traditions (For example, tragedy and farce, the conventional and the idiosyncratic, moralization and perversity) held together by a brilliant energy and characterized by a totally appropriate verse.

———. "*The Revenger's Tragedy*: Jacobean Dance of Death." *Modern Language Quarterly* 15 (1954), 201–7. An excellent description of how the traditional emblem of the Danse Macabre is related to the notions of sinful man and vengeful God in *The Revenger's Tragedy*.

4. Studies of *The Atheist's Tragedy*

HIGGINS, M. H. "The Influence of Calvinistic Thought in *The Atheist's Tragedy*." *Review of English Studies* 19 (1943), 255–62. Higgins finds the play Calvinistic in its disgust with physical human nature. Charlemont and Castabella are seen as ideal Puritan heroes.

LEECH, CLIFFORD. "*The Atheist's Tragedy* as a Dramatic Comment on Chapman's Bussy Plays." *Journal of English and Germanic Philology* 52 (1953), 525–30. Tourneur's play represents a "Christianization" of Chapman's themes in *Bussy D'Ambois* and *The Revenge of Bussy*.

LEVIN, RICHARD. "The Subplot of *The Atheist's Tragedy*." *Huntington Library Quarterly* 29 (1965), 17–33. A penetrating analysis of the complex relationships between the main plot, subplot, and a third, clown-level plot. All three work to the same thematic end, at different levels of seriousness.

ORNSTEIN, ROBERT. "*The Atheist's Tragedy* and Renaissance Naturalism." *Studies in Philology* 51 (1954), 194–207. Ornstein sees D'amville's view of nature as that of the archetypal Renaissance atheist.

5. History

While a complete bibliography of Renaissance history is, of course, impossible here, the following four works should prove helpful to the student of Tourneur. Two are general English histories, two are concerned with specific families with which Tourneur was associated.

BINDOFF, S. T. *Tudor England.* Baltimore: Penguin Books, 1950. An excellent general survey of England at the time of Tourneur's birth.

MARKHAM, C. R. *The Fighting Veres.* London: Sampson Low, 1888. A bit florid and old fashioned, but nevertheless the best full length portrait of the general who dominates Tourneur's early military career.

SMITH, L. B. "England's Second Family." *Horizon* 9 (1967), 68–79. An entertaining portrait of the Cecil family, from Elizabethan times to the present. Since Tourneur's relationship with the Cecils seems one of service more to the family than any particular person, this is a useful introduction to an extraordinary group.

TREVELYAN, G. M. *History of England,* vol. 2, *Tudors and The Stuart Era.* London: Longmans, Green, 1926. Still a classic liberal historical overview of Renaissance England.

Index

162